Schizophrenic
Women

Schizophrenic
Women
Studies in Marital Crisis

Harold Sampson
Sheldon L. Messinger
Robert D. Towne

With a new introduction by Rita J. Simon

with the collaboration of
David Ross
Florine Livson
Mary Bowers
Lester Cohen
Kate Dorst

Routledge
Taylor & Francis Group
LONDON AND NEW YORK

First published 2005 by Transaction Publishers

Published 2017 by Routledge
2 Park Square, Milton Park, Abingdon, Oxon, OX14 4RN
711 Third Avenue, New York, NY 10017, USA

Routledge is an imprint of the Taylor & Francis Group, an informa business

Library of Congress Catalog Number: 2005048526

Library of Congress Cataloging-in-Publication Data

Sampson, Harold.
Schizophrenic women : studies in marital crisis / Harold Sampson, Sheldon L. Messinger, and Robert D. Towne ; with a new introduction by Rita J. Simon.
p. cm.
Originally published: New York : Atherton Press, 1964, in series: The Atherton Press behavioral science series. With new introd.
Includes bibliographical references and index.
ISBN 0-202-30816-2 (pbk. : alk. paper)
1. Schizophrenia—Case studies. 2. Schizophrenics—Family relationships—Case studies. 3. Women—Mental health—Case studies.
I. Messinger, Sheldon L. II. Towne, Robert D. III. Title.

RC514.S313 2005
362.196'898'0082—dc22   2005048526

ISBN 13: 978-0-202-30816-6 (pbk)

Contents

Introduction to the
AldineTransaction Edition

Schizophrenic Women makes a valuable contribution to our under-standing of psychotic illness, intrafamily relations, the effectiveness of hospitalization, and the likelihood of complete recovery. It de-scribes the experiences of seventeen families in which the wife and, in some instances, the mother as well, is diagnosed as schizophrenic.

The study focuses not only on the patient but describes in detail the family (husband, maternal and paternal mothers, and children) interactions leading up to the crisis that results in hospitalization.

The authors interviewed the seventeen schizophrenic women, all of whom were admitted at least once to a California state mental hos-pital in the 1950s, their spouses, the maternal and paternal mothers, the hospital physicians, and in some instances private psychiatrists, over an extended period of time. The average number of interviews for each case was fifty. The interviews were conducted prior to hospi-talization, during hospitalization, and following hospitalization.

In addition to the in-depth interviews the study team had access to hospital and other medical records and the opportunity for exten-sive observations of the intrafamily dynamics. The authors use ficti-tious names to identify each of the families.

The wives ranged in age from twenty-six to forty; the husbands from twenty-four to forty-five years. The wives' mean age was thirty-two; the husbands' thirty-five. The women had between one and five children at home. The children's ages ranged from six months to sixteen years. With the exception of one of the wives, all had at least some high school education, and five had attended college. Three of the husbands had a grammar school education, four attended college, and two received postgraduate degrees. The authors characterize the families as belonging primarily to the upper-lower or lower-middle classes.

How the wives are transformed into mental patients is described in considerable detail. The authors emphasize that becoming a psychiatric patient is not a function simply of being mentally ill but is a socially structured event in which the relationships among the family members play a crucial role. Family ties become increasingly disrupted and in some instances are in permanent jeopardy.

The median length of stay in the state hospital was four months. During their hospitalization all of the women participated in discussion groups, many of them were given drugs, and ten underwent electroshock therapy. None of them were involved in individual psychotherapy. At least six of the women were hospitalized a second time within two years of their first release.

As of the last time the authors had contact with the subjects, seven women were not living in the marital home. Three subjects were, but had been separated at least once following their release from the hospital. Seven women were living in the same family situation continuously since their release. Of those ten women, eight were reported as relatively free of any overt psychotic symptoms.

The appendix provides detailed case studies of the seventeen subjects, including biographical details, data about the families' demographics, the changing nature and quality of the marital relationships, the ties to the subjects' mothers and mothers-in-law, specifics about the subjects' mental illness, the treatments they received, and an assessment of their current mental and family status.

Schizophrenic Women is an exhaustive and illuminating study of the lives of seventeen women who suffered severe psychosis and the treatment they received. It describes not only the forms their illness took but also their changing and disintegrating relationships primarily with their husbands and mothers. Although the study was conducted in the 1950s, readers will recognize its current relevance and importance for scholars and the lay public interested in the problem of mental illness and intrafamily relationships.

Rita J. Simon
University Professor
American University

Preface

This volume is based on the lives of seventeen families that suffered the experiences associated with the hospitalization of the
wife and mother for mental illness. A description and analysis of
representative experiences is presented in an attempt to provide
provisional answers to certain questions: What were the family
schemes of living—the base-line patterns of relatedness, strivings,
and adaptations—which preceded the crises leading to mental
hospitalization? How did these schemes of living fall apart? How
did personal and family crises become psychiatric emergencies?
To what extent and in what ways did hospital experiences
modify the immediate crises and the earlier schemes of living?
How durable were the reorganized schemes of living fashioned
during hospitalization as the patients again moved into the community? Throughout the report a persistent attempt has been
made to hold to the aim of placing mental hospitalization and
return to the community in the context of ongoing lives. We feel
that placing these events in this context is crucial to both understanding and affecting them in a controlled and therapeutic

manner. Because this perspective will be emphasized throughout the book, we shall say no more about it here.

But this book is about more than the immediate lives of seventeen women and their families. We have also directed attention to patterns of psychiatric care, to the ways in which such crises as those experienced by these women and their families come to professional attention and are then managed. We have sought to explore how help is found and used and some of the functions hospitalization serves for patients and their families. We have also been concerned to discern some of the ways that traditional patterns of psychiatric care limit our power to observe, understand, and effectively influence a pathological course of events.

The volume has been written in the hope that its subject matter will interest a wide and varied audience. Clinicians, administrators, and research workers concerned with understanding and caring for the mentally ill will find the report of most direct interest, but we have also aimed to present ideas of interest to social scientists concerned with analysis of the relations between individual stability and social institutions, particularly the family. Finally, we entertain the hope that some people not professionally concerned with human behavior but, like all of us, concerned to understand it, may find the report of interest.

The report draws on the several journal articles we have published on various aspects of the study. We should like to thank our various publishers for permission to use portions of these articles. Here we have attempted to bring our materials together in a unified conceptual scheme; we have also added materials not found in any of our published articles.

The study on which the report is based was carried out by an interdisciplinary group that functioned as an independent research unit in the California Department of Mental Hygiene. The members of the group were principally trained in psychology. Exceptions were Sheldon L. Messinger, a sociologist; Robert D. Towne, a psychiatrist; and Mary Bowers, a social worker. People from other disciplines—anthropology and statistics, for instance—acted as occasional advisers to the group.

We should like to note that at no time in the course of the

study was there any attempt by the California Department of Mental Hygiene or its staff to influence the direction of our work. Once having decided that the work was worth doing, a strictly hands-off policy was followed. We should like to record our high regard for the department and its staff, as well as our gratitude to them, especially Leon J. Epstein, Richard D. Morgan, Robert T. Ross, and Nathan Sloate, who, during the course of the study, were members of the department's headquarters staff, for the moral, administrative, and technical help each extended to us.

Our work was principally supported by a grant (3M-9124) from the National Institute of Mental Health. We are, of course, grateful for this support and for the encouragement and help we received from individual staff members of NIMH. The original impetus for the work grew out of conversations in late 1956 between John A. Clausen, then chief of the Laboratory of Socioenvironmental Studies, and the first author. At the time Dr. Clausen and his associates were conducting a series of groundbreaking studies of the careers and family lives of married male mental patients, and the idea emerged of similarly studying married female mental patients. Morton Kramer, chief of the Biometrics Branch, was also most helpful in these early, as well as later, discussions, as was Richard H. Williams, chief of the Professional Services Branch. Dr. Williams consulted with us throughout the study. He read and provided us with valuable comments on memoranda and working drafts; finally, he was kind enough to read an early version of this report.

Many other people contributed to the development and accomplishment of this study and report. At various stages we received formal and informal counsel from Gregory Bateson, Harold Garfinkel, Erving Goffman, Portia Bell Hume, Don D. Jackson, John I. Kitsuse, Timothy Leary, Henry Maas, Rodney Prestwood, David Schneider, Tamotsu Shibutani, and Ozzie G. Simmons. We are most appreciative. We should also like to thank Dorothy Bilinski, Gloria Neal, and Deanna Miller for help in running an office while transcribing thousands of pages of materials and in managing to know where everything was.

We are deeply indebted to the cooperation of many persons

on the staff of the state mental hospital where much of our work took place. Only our concern for carrying through our pledge of confidentiality of sources and anonymity of patients and family members prevents us from mentioning them by name. The same is true of the staffs of local bureaus of social work, which provide aftercare to Department of Mental Hygiene patients, and the many private practitioners and public and private community agencies who helped us by freely giving of their time and recollections.

Most of all, we are strongly and personally indebted to the patients and family members who consented to talk with us about their lives, fully knowing that we could not offer them direct services other than an attempt to hear and understand their often painful experiences. All of them shared with us the hope that the study might cast light on problems of importance to them and many others. We hope that this has been accomplished in however small measure. We have, of course, protected their anonymity by using fictitious code names and by altering such identifying data as age, occupation, and geographical residence.

As is the case with any genuine collaboration, it is difficult after a while to locate the exact sources of ideas and to separate elaboration from origination. We trust that we have noted in the report the sources of ideas outside the research group itself. Within the group, we gave up the attempt. The order in which we have listed names reflects the joint evaluation of the three senior authors of individual contributions to the conceptualization, research, and writing that went into the study. The actual writing of this final report was primarily the responsibility of the project director, Harold Sampson, but was based on published and unpublished articles and memoranda prepared by all three senior authors during the course of the work, as well as interviews, field notes, memoranda, and summaries prepared by the five junior authors.

We must note here, with sorrow, that our colleague and friend, Robert D. Towne, died before the final editing of the report was completed. We did have the benefit of his comments on the first draft of the report, however, and we have tried to take his recommendations into account. We believe he would have approved of the result.

Harold Sampson
Sheldon L. Messinger

1964
Berkeley, California

In memory of Robert D. Towne, M.D.

1

The Crisis and Its Context

Concept and Approach

This report describes a critical period in the lives of seventeen married women and their families. Some time during the 1950's each of these women was admitted as a patient to a California state mental hospital and therein diagnosed as schizophrenic. Their ties to their intimates had become tenuous and fraught with intense, disturbing emotions and fantasies. They were very withdrawn—in most instances confused and delusional, in some instances suffering from terrifying hallucinations. The immediate past and present were frightening, painful, confused, and unreal, and no predictable and tolerable future could be convincingly envisioned. Their everyday world and their customary, implicit scheme of living had shattered.

For some, the episode had occurred suddenly, with well-defined boundaries. For others, the episode had developed so gradually that it would be difficult to say when the person would first have seemed clinically schizophrenic. This was the first state mental hospitalization for each of them, although one woman had been hospitalized in a private sanitarium for a month shortly before entering the state institution and two others had been patients in the psychiatric ward of a county hospital for a few days some time before the present crisis.

The critical period with which we are concerned did not begin with hospitalization, nor did it end with subsequent release. These women had experienced repeated severe difficulties over the years in their marital families. In time, these difficulties became unmanageable for them or their intimates, and the women were removed or removed themselves from the family setting. The hospitalization itself acknowledged and confirmed the collapse of earlier personal and family adaptations. During hospitalization, new personal and family adaptations were tentatively evolved. The period following the young woman's release from the hospital tested these tentative reorganizations and often further modified them.

The period we shall attempt to describe encompasses a sequence of organization-disorganization-reorganization. We shall trace in some detail the development of the crises which led to the admission of these women to the state mental hospital and the ways in which these crises were modified during hospitalization and following release. Our broad aim is to describe this extended segment of the careers of these women and their marital families and to understand these careers as shaped by and as parts of family and institutional processes.

Our emphasis on this broad sweep of time and events cuts across traditional patterns of psychiatric care and traditional conceptions which have developed in relation to these patterns. The career of the mental patient and his family has typically come to the attention of treatment personnel during an emergency and then faded when the emergency was in some way resolved. The patterns of living which precede the psychiatric emergency and which follow its immediate resolution have remained for the most part outside of the practitioner's field of observation. In addition, the professional people who become engaged with the future patient and his family before hospitalization seldom maintain their contact through hospitalization and afterward. Those responsible for hospital care rarely have any professional base in the outside community, and posthospital care, if any, falls to new hands. These compartmentalized arrangements have defined and limited therapeutic perspectives and have tended to segregate our conceptions about, as well as our treatment of, the prehospital, hospital, and posthospital phases of the crisis.

But patterns of treating such psychiatric problems are in great flux, and the trend is toward a more community-oriented management. The large, geographically distant, and administratively unwieldy state mental institution is yielding some of its prospective patients and some of its functions to the local general hospital and the specialized day-care or night-care facility. In these facilities care is provided nearer home, for briefer periods, and with more flexibility. Increasingly, the large mental institution is seeking organizational flexibility, giving explicit attention to the social milieu as a therapeutic (and antitherapeutic) force, and taking steps to reduce barriers between hospital and community. Increased attention is given to early release, aftercare, and also to early identification and treatment of emotional difficulties before they become unmanageable in the community. The concept of continuity of care receives some substance in plans to establish comprehensive mental health centers.[1]

These trends give practical point to our concern with describing and conceptualizing a critical period which is not bounded by hospitalization or release. The traditional mental hospital has been, for the most part, a passive recipient of its clients, having only a limited veto power over the entire process whereby a member of the community becomes subject to its care. There has been no question of choosing a time and strategy of intervention in terms of concepts of optimal accessibility to effective help. Usually, indeed, the hospital has been a last resort; thus, hospitalization has taken place when opportunities for

---

[1] These trends and the issues they pose are discussed in Richard H. Williams, ed., *The Prevention of Disability in Mental Disorders* (Mental Health Monograph I [Washington, D.C.: U.S. Department of Health, Education, and Welfare, n.d.]).

intervention were least promising.[2] After the patient's release the traditional mental hospital has had very limited scope for therapeutic activity. In this kind of institutional setting, interest in the details of the patient's extramural career is inevitably somewhat academic. The more earnestly treatment reaches out into the community, the more valuable knowledge of longitudinal patterns becomes. Strategies for earlier detection and intervention require knowledge about the precipitation of crises associated with the high risk of a serious psychiatric outcome, the ways in which such crises are ordinarily contained, and the circumstances under which they tend to become emergencies. We also need to know as much as possible about the determinants of seeking or avoiding professional help in such crises. These kinds of information can permit us to plan how to gear interventions to special opportunities or special risks.

We have considered the *post*hospital period not alone, as a social transition from one distinctive setting to another, but specifically, as a sequel to the personal and family crisis which resulted in hospitalization. The more usual approach in practice, research, and conceptualization is to emphasize discontinuities rather than continuities between the posthospital and prehospital experience. Because of his recent experience and current status, the patient may encounter such special problems as social stigma or finding himself locked out of former personal and vocational roles. The family, also, may have to accommodate itself to the management of a behaviorally deviant and emotionally disturbed person. In practice, there has been very little continuity of treatment, and the aftercare worker, if there is one, first encounters the patient and family to consult about posthospital issues.

Trends toward earlier prehospital care, briefer hospitalizations, and community hospital settings will inevitably modify the separateness of the posthospital period. The patient and family will experience relative continuity of care instead of a phase of

2 Harold Sampson, David Ross, Bernice Engle, and Florine Livson, "Feasibility of Community Clinic Treatment for State Mental Hospital Patients," *American Medical Association Archives of Neurology and Psychiatry,* LXXX (1958), 71–77.

relative isolation followed by a phase of attempted reintegration. The professional worker in comprehensive treatment facilities will have opportunities to observe and deal with the broad sweep of the crisis and its resolution, rather than a discrete phase of it. These changes will, we believe, emphasize the importance of forming a conception of the entire organization-disorganization-reorganization sequence and will stimulate further work using temporal units similar to those we have selected.

We shall not limit our description to the careers of patients alone, but will seriously attempt to characterize family adaptations, family crises, and family as well as personal solutions to crises. In this endeavor, also, our emphasis will tend to cut across many traditional concerns and modes of analysis, but will have particular significance to emerging patterns in the management of mental illness.

The large, geographically distant mental institution not only isolated the patient from his family, but at the same time effectively isolated those who treated him from the family setting in which the crisis arose and to which the patient was likely to return. The mental hospital practitioner met and treated his patients in an insular and semiautonomous province. It was only at the social boundaries of the province—admission, release, and visits—that he was compelled to deal with those who formed the immediate outside community of his patient. This historic pattern is undergoing change in both practice and research, and attention to family processes has become fashionable if not yet traditional. All trends toward an "open" hospital with early and frequent visiting and passes and short hospitalization for only the acute phase, with possible subsequent care, inevitably compel practitioners to become aware of and to relate to the patient's family. It is therefore predictable that family processes will become a matter of increasingly genuine, practical concern to a great many staff members in mental hospitals over the next years. They will come to require conceptions which link family structure and processes to their own therapeutic and administrative tasks.

There has been a great deal of research on family processes

and schizophrenia.[3] For the most part, it has been concerned primarily with the parental family and with the early development of those behavior patterns and psychic structures presumed to underlie later manifest illness. The parental family is generally recognized as the strategic site for personality development. Our own emphasis on the contemporary family setting of the chronologically mature individual assumes that *it* is a strategic site for personality stabilization or decompensation in adult life. This assumption is particularly justifiable for the group of women studied. It was an intended product of our sample selection procedures that all the women were wives and mothers at the time of hospitalization. It was empirically true that none was regularly employed outside the home in the period shortly preceding hospitalization, and it also turned out that very few had ever had significant adult involvements in the occupational sphere. Thus family roles provided their main tie to participation in communal reality and their main immediate source of gratification and threat.

The contemporary marital family might be expected, then, to have importance in the development of the wife's schizophrenic crisis in two related ways. First, participation in the marital family would press strategic demands, activating earlier developmental conflicts and uncovering earlier developmental defects. Second, the adaptation of the wife to these demands and conflicts would be shaped by the concrete organization of marital family life fashioned from the interlocking anxieties, conflicts, and conditions of intimacy in the family group. Her personal adaptations would be shaped by and be part of a family adaptation. These family adaptations, we assumed, could mitigate or intensify the personal conflicts of the wives. The eventual collapse of her personal adaptation must then be linked in an intrinsic, rather than a merely incidental, way to the collapse of a pre-existing pattern of family adaptation.

The contemporary family situation might also be expected to be of importance in determining when and how treatment was sought and hospitalization utilized. It is known that people who

---

[3] See, for example, Don D. Jackson, ed., *The Etiology of Schizophrenia* (New York: Basic Books, Inc., 1960), Part VI, pp. 323–440.

are severely impaired in their functioning or even overtly psychotic may remain in the community for a long time without being identified as psychiatrically ill and without professional treatment.[4] During this period, the disturbed person maintains some type of accommodative pattern with his immediate personal community. This pattern permits or forces him to remain in the community in spite of his severe difficulties. In the cases studied, as is frequently true, the immediate personal community is the family; thus the family serves as the typical proximate agency of social control and forms a critical boundary between the individual and more formal means of social control. Professional help and intervention become important when and as family mechanisms of control are experienced as inadequate. We thus assumed that a careful investigation of family processes in relation to seeking professional help and deciding to hospitalize the patient would be essential to understanding how a personal or family crisis becomes a psychiatric emergency.

Finally, the contemporary family situation might be expected to be of importance in shaping the resolution of the prehospital crisis. The reorganization of the patient's shattered scheme of living must include either a repair of disrupted family relationships or the establishment of alternative ties to the community. Any changes in family relationships promoted by the crisis and hospitalization would inevitably influence, as well as be influenced by, the patient's psychic reorganization. The adjustment tasks and possibilities encountered by the patient after release, as well as his likelihood of remaining in the community, are in part determined by the interpersonal setting to which he returns.[5]

These considerations led us to commit a formidable amount of research time and effort to the study of marital families. We

[4] Marion Radke Yarrow, Charlotte Green Schwartz, Harriet S. Murphy, and Leila Calhoun Deasy, "The Psychological Meaning of Mental Illness in the Family," *The Journal of Social Issues*, XI, No. 4 (1955), 12–24.

[5] Ozzie G. Simmons and Howard E. Freeman, "Familial Expectations and Posthospital Performance of Mental Patients," *Human Relations*, XII, No. 3 (1959), 233–242; Freeman and Simmons, *The Mental Patient Comes Home* (New York: John Wiley & Sons, Inc., 1963).

sought as much information as possible about the backgrounds of the husbands as well as of the patients. Ongoing interaction processes were observed and conceptualized, and detailed histories of the marital families were obtained. We tried to learn how professional agents and hospital processes wittingly and unwittingly modified family life.

This report, then, is concerned with various levels of crisis and with relationships between these levels. There is, first, the personal crisis of the patient—the collapse of her defensive and adaptive patterns, resulting in the shattering experience of psychosis, subsequent mental hospitalization, and a partial recovery which may consolidate or decay as she picks up the threads of her life. A second level is that of the family crisis—the failure of those defensive and adaptive arrangements instituted in the marital family to meet requisites of family life and needs of individual participants, resulting in an unmanageable emergency, removal of the wife from the family setting, and then tentative reorganizations which may or may not survive testing by subsequent experiences. Finally, there is the level of the public psychiatric crisis, which arises only as personal distress and deviance is brought to the attention of the wider community and defined as a serious psychiatric problem, thereby invoking new mechanisms of control and new sets of role expectations for family members.

METHODS

The decision to follow what would inevitably be a small number of patients and their families over an extended time and to reconstruct for each case the vicissitudes of a crisis was most compatible with a broad, exploratory method of investigation. We could not expect to test previously stated propositions nor to obtain reliable statistics about characteristics of a defined population. We could expect, however, to locate hypothetically important processes and relationships if we exploited the special if restricted virtues of this approach. The particular opportunity afforded by an exploratory study is that of flexibility—data-collection procedures may be modified by new insights or hunches; the research lens may be wide-angle at one moment and adjust for close-ups at the next; and analytic questions and hypotheses may be allowed to develop gradually out of wide experience. We did, in fact, decide at various choice points to pursue an interesting lead or unexpected observation even when this meant that data across cases would not be uniform.

The research team was a specially constituted interdisciplinary group without formal affiliation to any treatment institution. We had no responsibility for administrative or treatment decisions. We worked out an explicit arrangement to obtain information from hospital personnel and other officials while withholding the content of our interviews and observations from them. We observed but did not participate in such decision-making processes as the release conference. We also exercised restraint with patients and their families in directly intervening to offer information, advice, and interpretations. All of our informants were explicitly informed that we were engaged in research, kept our data confidential, and did not contribute to treatment decisions. We held to this definition whatever other role assignments our informants attempted to grant us in fantasy or practice.

This observational role helped us to gain access to kinds of data not ordinarily available to people in other positions in the social system. For example, we regularly obtained information from patients and spouses about postrelease plans which they withheld from hospital personnel because they knew (or supposed) that such information would influence the likelihood of the patients' release. Thus, the Bakers informed us of divorce plans which were deliberately concealed from the hospital staff. At the same time, our research role prevented us from testing hunches against experience by deliberately intervening in a situation and observing the consequences. Alfred H. Stanton and Morris S. Schwartz have well discussed the advantages of such interventions in distinguishing merely plausible from effective causes of an observed phenomenon.[6] Further, our research role

6 Alfred H. Stanton and Morris S. Schwartz, *The Mental Hospital* (New York: Basic Books, Inc., 1954), pp. 428–429.

limited access to certain kinds of data the psychotherapist might obtain in extended contact with patients and spouses. This limitation, however, requires qualification in two important ways.

First, the peculiarities of our role permitted us to maintain contact over a long time with patients and spouses who would have avoided, and did avoid, involvement with treatment personnel. We were thus able to bring into quasi-systematic research observation some of that large group of people who do not appear—except transiently at the height of an emergency—in the office of the physician, psychiatrist, or aftercare social worker. Those who do become involved in a continuing treatment before or after hospitalization are a special and atypical subgroup of the larger population. Second, we explicitly recognized that we could not maintain contact with patients and spouses without in some way giving them something (interest, information, clarifications) and without becoming important figures (e.g., identification objects) in their lives. Each research relationship was routinely reviewed with Robert D. Towne, the psychiatrist on the research staff. In practice, some research relationships moved toward a level of trust and comfort which permitted us to gain significant access to both private and covert experience. Such relationships became important to our informants and provided them with genuine support in coping with their severe difficulties. In other instances, the relationships remained minimal and guarded and provided us with only a gross picture of the changing lives of our informants.

It would be misleading to view our method of investigation as yielding a simple "natural history" of a crisis and its resolution. One cannot remain outside the field of forces while forming relationships with informants. We have tried to use the research contact to illuminate rather than obscure the major forces—intrapsychic, interpersonal, and institutional—which influenced the vicissitudes of the crisis.

Selection of Cases

The size of the study group was limited by our preferred emphasis on longitudinal issues, the choice of a broad exploratory approach, and the commitment to describe family relationships and institutional processes. We chose to make the study group as homogeneous as possible along certain dimensions. Homogeneity of cases would make it easier to obtain relatively uniform data across families and would facilitate discovery of ordering principles in a small sample through the replication of similar instances. The dimensions on which homogeneity was sought reflect the central interest areas of the study.

We invoked, first, a set of criteria intended to provide gross uniformity in family structure, most particularly in the roles occupied by the patients prior to hospitalization. Families were selected through white female patients who were, at the time of admission, married, living with their husbands,[7] forty years of age or under, and the mother of one or more dependent children (under eighteen) in the home. These criteria were intended to select "practicing" white wife-mothers of child-rearing age and their families.

We also required that the wives be diagnosed as schizophrenic by the hospital. This criterion was intended to provide gross uniformity in the nature and severity of the problems the wives experienced and presented to the family, as well as in the socially validated interpretation of these problems.

Another set of criteria was intended to control the experiences of family members with community resources for dealing with severe mental illness. We required that the wives have no previous hospitalization for mental illness and no previous outpatient treatment with electroshock therapy. After some valuable time and effort had been invested in three cases, it was learned that the wives had had previous brief hospitalizations for psychiatric complaints. One woman had been hospitalized for a month in a private sanitarium earlier in the same year as her admission to the state mental institution; the other two had been in the psychiatric ward of a county hospital for a few days some years

---

[7] In the Arlen case there was a separation about a week before hospitalization, presumably to simplify care of Mrs. Arlen and the children during a chaotic period. In several cases, as our exposition will show, the issue of marital separation was prominent just prior to hospitalization.

earlier. We decided to retain these wives and their families in the study group.

In order to control the point at which we entered the scene, as well as to select that point most relevant for our purposes, we required that the wives be newly admitted and that contact with patient and spouse be initiated by a research staff member immediately thereafter.

Finally, we required that the wives be hospitalized in a state mental institution near research headquarters and that the residence of the family be about an hour's automobile ride from our office. These criteria were invoked primarily for our own convenience.

The wives were to be selected consecutively from the stream of incoming patients. Actually, a few women who met all criteria had to be skipped because no staff member was available to begin to see them immediately after their admission.

Seventeen families were studied. Selection of wives and their families ended when our resources for seeing cases were spent. Seventeen families thus represent the maximum number that could be followed by our case methods in the available time. The number of families has no other procedural significance. It is obvious that a few more cases would not have greatly modified our limited base for generalization. We believe that very many fewer cases would have obscured the range of variability in some of the processes studied.

A "case" consisted of a variable number of informants beyond the wife-patient. The ambiguous boundaries of our cases were a predictable product of one of the tasks we set ourselves— exploring in some detail the designs and limits of the interpersonal networks in which our patients were, or became, embedded during the immediate prehospital, hospital, and immediate posthospital periods. The minimum number of informants necessary to constitute a case for our purposes was the patient herself; her spouse; the hospital physicians involved in the patient's admission, treatment, ward assignments, and release; and other personnel implicated in these same processes. Other informants varied for four broad reasons. Some cases included important participants, such as a private psychiatrist, not present in other cases. Some important participants were geographically inaccessible, such as a mother living in another state. Still other participants we regarded as psychologically or socially inaccessible, such as the next-door neighbors or a community physician in the absence of a release of information. Finally, certain possibly important participants were excluded by choice on the principle that it was not feasible to see everyone and that we must focus on the patient-family nexus and official incursions on it.

The members of our study group all moved through one state hospital, which we selected primarily for our own convenience, but also because it seemed fairly typical of state institutions at the time the study was conducted. The institution housed about five thousand patients. As with similar institutions, a large number of the patients were elderly or chronic, and another large number were acute and tended to be released to the community in a few months of admission. Trained psychiatrists were in short supply, and those on hand typically were in administrative or supervisory roles. Although tranquilizing drugs were used in the wards studied, the dosage was small and seemed to be principally conceived of as a substitute for sedatives. Individual psychotherapy was nearly nonexistent except for a few patients involved in special projects. Group and milieu therapies were in widespread vogue, but in the informal usage of many staff members as well as patients, the word "treatment" literally and exclusively meant electroshock therapy.

Most members of the study group encountered certain typical categories of remedial agents during the immediate prehospital and posthospital phases of their careers. For example, a community physician and psychiatrist were usually involved in the pathway to the mental hospital. In most cases we were able to obtain a release of information from patients and family members and interview and review the records of both typical and idiosyncratic remedial agents involved with study group families.

Our study of seventeen patients involved us with over one hundred direct informants, not counting state hospital personnel.

Of these, however, routine interviewing over an extended period was limited to patients and spouses.

Various characteristics of the study group families are presented in case studies in the Appendix. A few summary remarks here may prove useful to the reader, however.

The wives ranged in age from twenty-six to forty years at time of admission; their mean age was about thirty-two. The husbands' ages ranged from twenty-four to forty-five years, averaging about thirty-five. Nine of the wives had been married to their current husbands from two to ten years; eight, from eleven to sixteen years. Five wives had been previously married; this was true of two husbands. The wives had from one to five children at home, and the children's ages ranged from six months to sixteen years.

Most of the families had incomes of less than $7,000 a year, but the annual income of one family was close to $10,000 and of another more than $15,000. All but one wife had at least some high school education, and five had gone to college for a time or had nurse's training beyond high school graduation. Three of the husbands had only grammar school education; four had gone to college, and two of these had received postgraduate degrees. Thus there is some range in the socioeconomic characteristics of the group, but most cases fell into the upper-lower or lower-middle classes.

Three wives did not see a psychiatrist even for evaluation prior to hospitalization. Ten others saw a psychiatrist one or more times during the emergency preceding admission; four had entered a treatment contact of eight, sixteen, thirty-one, and sixty-six sessions respectively.

Eleven wives were admitted to the hospital by the courts; six were self-admitted. Their mean stay in the state hospital from admission to first release was about nineteen weeks. One stayed only six weeks, another stayed sixty-four weeks. None of the women received individual psychotherapy at the hospital; all received relatively small and intermittent dosages of tranquilizing drugs. Ten of the seventeen received electroshock therapy at some time during their hospital stay.

Data-Collection

The aims of data-collection were to build up, through interviews, observation, and abstraction of pertinent records, detailed descriptions of the wives' and husbands' backgrounds and marital careers, the crises preceding hospitalization, the wives' course of hospitalization, and the posthospital conduct of and relations between members of the seventeen study group families.

One interviewer was responsible, under supervision, for the collection of all materials pertinent to a case. Coverage of particular events, topics, and processes were specified in field data guides and memos, but many of these were prepared subsequent to the collection of a substantial portion of the data. These guides and memos also tended to be overinclusive on the one hand and insufficiently attuned to the interpersonal rhythms of interviewing on the other. The major device for achieving relatively adequate and uniform coverage was the weekly staff conference and individual supervisory sessions.

With the exception of the staff sociologist, all interviewers had had some training and experience in clinical work in psychiatric settings. All cases were routinely reviewed with the staff psychiatrist from the point of view of understanding and resolving relational problems between interviewer and informants. No formal measuring instruments were employed. The main method of investigation was the semistructured interview, but field observations and records data were also used. We routinely obtained a variety of hospital records—for example, ward chart entries, social histories, financial accounts, correspondence, treatment records, conference summaries, restraint and seclusion records, visit cards and records, reports of psychiatric and medical examinations, and special incident reports.

We were often able to obtain releases of information from the patient and family members, thus achieving access to records from various community agents involved in the case before or after hospitalization. These data were supplemented by direct interviews with the people involved in the incident, event, treatment, or other contact. Interview and records data pertained directly to the study group. Field observations described selected hospital processes—ward meetings and the release conference—which our patients encountered, but our interest here was directed toward the achievement of a more general understanding of the way these processes operate, the functions they may serve for hospital personnel, and the impact they may be expected to have on patients and family members.

The wife-patients and their husbands were each interviewed regularly and frequently from admission up to more than one hundred weeks after the wives' releases from the mental hospital. The interviews were partially structured and ran from about thirty minutes to two hours in length, averaging slightly over an hour. The majority of interviews were reconstructed from notes and dictated by the interviewer soon after the session, but in about half the cases there is one or more tape recorded interviews with the wife, the husband, or both.

The number of interviews with wives and husbands ranged from about thirty-five to about seventy for each case; the mean number for each case was about fifty interviews. In most cases it was possible to schedule one or more joint interviews during which interaction between husband and wife could be directly observed.

Husbands were usually interviewed at home while the wives were in the hospital, and in the posthospital period husbands and wives were seen when possible in their homes. To achieve maximum participation, we conducted interviews wherever and whenever convenient for our informants. Thus, for example, some interviews were conducted during the lunch hour near the husband's place of work.

Early in our work we established a hypothetical schedule of desired frequency of contact with the marital partners. The schedule was based on the wish to form a stable relationship, to achieve access to relatively private experience, and to keep on top of processes of interest to us. The schedule called for us to conduct about three interviews every four weeks with the patient and two every four weeks with the husband during the hospital period. This frequency would continue through the first twelve posthospital weeks, then gradually diminish, until after the first posthospital year, for example, frequency would approximate one interview every eight weeks with each of the marital partners.

This hypothetical schedule bears a gross relationship to our actual experience as expressed in average number of interviews achieved during four-week time units during different career phases. But deviations from it, planned and otherwise, were quite common. We sought more frequent interviews during particular crises. We missed desired interviews for trivial reasons (e.g., the interviewer had a cold) or serious reasons (e.g., the informant was unwilling to see us or had moved away).

Over-all, we found it easier to establish and maintain contact with patient and spouse over extended periods than we had at first anticipated. Fairly typically, but not universally, we encountered less interest in and more resistance to participation with us during the posthospital than the hospital period. We believe this reflects a characteristic attempt to isolate and forget the illness and the hospital period after release.

The wives were a captive audience during the hospital period, and many of them were appreciative of any outside contact even during the acute phase of their episode. It was usually possible to maintain any desired frequency of contact with the wives during the hospital period although we were not always able to maintain desired frequency of contact and breadth of coverage with wives following their release. In only one of the seventeen cases, however, did the wife flatly refuse to continue to see us after release. In this instance, we had to rely exclusively on the limited information about the posthospital period made available to us by the Bureau of Social Work and the statistical research unit of the Department of Mental Hygiene. In three other instances the wives moved out of the area after several posthospital months. In two of these cases, our relationship to the marital partners was excellent, and we were able to maintain some further contact through correspondence and to visit them for a final posthospital interview about two years after release. In the third case, the wife was rehospitalized in another state, but shipped back to California, and it was possible at that time to obtain further interviews and to study rehospitalization records.

The husbands were also generally cooperative during the

hospital period, with mild to substantial decline in availability and involvement during the posthospital period. Those husbands who were in process of separating from or divorcing their wives were an exception to the generally high level of cooperation. One husband who was divorcing his wife refused to participate after a single interview, and in this case our data came almost exclusively from the wife. It was also true of this case that husband-wife contact was minimal during the hospital period and entirely absent after her release. In three other instances where the husband and wife separated, we eventually lost routine contact with the husband. In one other case we did not obtain the husband's consent to see us until well along in the hospital period.

All patients and family members are identified by fictitious code names in order to protect their anonymity. The code names are identical to those already used by us in earlier publications of this study.

We have also taken the liberty of introducing alterations in such identifying data as age, occupation, prior geographical residence, and the like. These alterations were carefully selected to preserve as well as possible the basic elements of the patient's life situation, while affording some further safeguards of anonymity.

These methods of data-collection enabled us to obtain variable but frequently impressive access to the prehospital adult lives of the patients and their spouses, to ongoing interaction processes in these families, and to the impact of institutional processes on family relationships. The raw data consisted of well over ten thousand double-spaced typewritten pages of interviews, records, and field observations.

The basic filing system constituted a preliminary sorting of materials. All materials, except field observations of hospital processes not directly involving our study group, were filed by case and, within cases, by informants. We used topical headings —"concerns about stigma," "posthospital anticipations"—to some extent in interviews, but, unfortunately, with too much variation to permit the use of these headings as an adequate guide to the location of specific topics.

The primary reduction of this rich but unruly material was

accomplished by a detailed event chronology by case. These chronologies, prepared by the interviewer responsible for the case, summarized by date all information known to us, from any source, about events in the lives of patient and spouse. The chronologies were indexed; that is, they specified the location and source of the material abstracted. In the nature of our work, with its multiple informants and length of contact, a given incident (e.g., first contact with a community psychiatrist) may have a dozen references scattered through the interviews and records. The chronology would summarize the perspectives of each participant and index all raw materials bearing on the event. The staff member preparing the chronology would also summarize his own observations and impressions about the case: developmental histories, background and development of the prehospital crisis, patterns of family interaction, and changes in patient and family during the hospital period and subsequently. These summaries were also carefully indexed.

A series of other forms summarized social and psychological background by case. Besides routine information—employment histories, kinship network—these forms provided space for indication by the interviewers of any salient relations to be found in a case. The course of the wives' hospitalization—ward movements, medication, passes, and the like—was also summarized on a special form.

The analysis proper relied on these summary documents and on frequent reference to the indexed primary materials. Analysis consisted of detailed examination of longitudinal sequences and interaction patterns and induction of the common features of diverse concrete instances. This is the "documentary method" of the social sciences and is, of course, closely akin to the clinical-inductive method in psychiatry and psychology. It exploits detailed, rich, complex longitudinal data, but is inherently subjective in selection, emphasis, and interpretation of data. It was the method deemed appropriate to the "soft" data and broad exploratory aims of the investigation.

2

Mary Yale

Crises of Separation

A critical time in normal development and in pathology is when the young person attempts to leave home and assume the responsibilities and prerogatives of adult life.[1] It presents opportunities for further growth and integration and corresponding dangers of identity diffusion, stagnation, or serious crisis. The special importance of the tasks of transition posed by this period for the development of schizophrenic crises has been given explicit emphasis by Theodore Lidz and Stephen Fleck, who "have considered schizophrenia to be essentially an illness of adolescence and early adult life even when the manifest illness appears later."[2] It is at this period of life that some people suffer a schizophrenic episode as they attempt to function as an adult. Other schizophrenic types frequently described in the psychiatric liter-

---

[1] This chapter is based in part on our earlier article, "Two Types of Schizophrenic Crises in Women," and portions of the article are reprinted with permission from the *Bulletin of the Menninger Clinic*, XXV (1961), 296–306. Copyright 1961 by the Menninger Foundation.

[2] Theodore Lidz and Stephen Fleck, "Schizophrenia, Human Integration, and the Role of the Family," in Jackson, *op. cit.*, pp. 323–345.

20

ature barely attempt even a limited transition beyond infantile objects and childhood roles and as adults remain bound almost exclusively in an intense symbiotic relationship with their mothers.

There is, however, a substantial proportion of patients who suffer their first recognized schizophrenic episode as young adults living in marital families. This is particularly true for female schizophrenics. In a statistical survey the authors found that, of all schizophrenic first admissions to four California state mental hospitals during a twelve-month period (1953–1954), 55 per cent of the women patients were married at the time of admission; 24 per cent of these women were classified as divorced, separated, or widowed. In this sample the corresponding proportion of men married at the time of admission was 29 per cent, and only 18 per cent were classified as divorced, separated, or widowed.

Thus the small group of women we have studied is representative in regard to family setting at time of admission of a sizable number of first-admission female schizophrenics. The group is of particular interest in more than this quantitative sense. It provides a contrast to that more frequently described situation in which the patient has remained in the parental home and has failed to achieve any significant formal participation in adult roles. In the majority of studies concerned with the link between family processes and the pathology of the patient, the index case has been, at the time of observation, an incumbent of roles primarily in his family of orientation. The contrasting composition of our group provides a strategic opportunity to investigate aspects of the conflict experienced by many schizophrenics in moving beyond childhood roles and objects and attempting to function as adults. This is because for our cases such steps as leaving the parental home, establishing a marital relationship, and bearing and rearing children have been actually undertaken, and the conflicts posed by such transitions may thus become manifest. At the contrasting extreme—for example, in the all-encompassing mother-daughter symbioses described by David Limentani—few real attempts to move toward participation in adult roles may be discerned, and the ordinary transitional crises of adolescence and young adulthood are muted.[3]

The women we studied did experience massive and repetitive difficulties in meeting tasks of transition. This was true of cases in which the episode occurred suddenly with well-defined boundaries, as well as of cases in which the episode developed so gradually that it would be difficult to say when the person would first have seemed clinically schizophrenic. These women encountered insurmountable inner and outer obstacles in attempting to accomplish and sustain a movement into adult roles in marital families of their own. They thus resemble those people characterized by Freud as falling ill of a developmental process which requires them to transform earlier fixations in order to fulfill new requisitions in reality. "The change for which such patients strive, but which they achieve only imperfectly or not at all, is regularly equivalent to a step forward for them in real life."[4]

In studying series of events in the lives of these patients and their contemporary families, we began to identify certain gross uniformities in the types of transitional crises experienced by different cases. The first pattern of crisis, which we shall designate a crisis of separation, will be introduced by a detailed excerpt from the adult life of Mary Yale. The presentation will include descriptions of family processes and processes associated with treatment and becoming hospitalized which go beyond our immediate theme, but foreshadow the concerns of subsequent chapters.

THE YALES

At the age of twenty-four Mary Yale left her widowed mother for the first time, moved to a distant city, and within the month married a man she had not previously known. Mary had

---

[3] David Limentani, "Symbiotic Identification in Schizophrenia," *Psychiatry*, XIX (1956), 231–236.

[4] Sigmund Freud, "Types of Neurotic Nosogenesis," in *Collected Papers* (London: Hogarth, 1924) II, 113–121; 116–117.

been living alone with her mother, Mrs. Brown, in a small apartment since the time of her father's death, when she was in her late teens. Both women worked. The young woman had a few girl friends and occasional casual dates with men. Her work was semiprofessional and of some interest to her, but she could not decide whether to continue in it or to seek additional schooling. Mrs. Brown did all the housework and cooking, washed her daughter's clothes, and even washed her hair. Mrs. Brown seemed to enjoy and to count on being helpful to her daughter, and she repeatedly emphasized the importance of family loyalty and the natural tendency to want to be very close to one's "own flesh and blood." In this relationship Mary seemed unable to assume much responsibility, to do much for herself, or to acquire firm involvements in the larger world. Mary later offered this account of her departure from home and marriage:

> I felt caught, and I had to get away from there. When I came to San Francisco, I wanted to go to college, yet it was also because I felt I had to get away from home. I think my first memory here is being scared, feeling alone. That's when I met George. I wasn't thinking seriously about marriage when we were married. I think I was—let's say I was—in revolt.

At the time of her marriage, then, Mary Yale was a twenty-four-year-old woman struggling to break away from her mother.

George Yale was a twenty-nine-year-old bachelor who "always thought I never would get married" and who had been successfully shying away from serious involvements with women. His mother lived across the country, and George acknowledged little obligation to or involvement with her. He saw himself as someone who with effort had managed to break away from a clinging and possessive mother. His father had divorced his mother during his childhood, and George had had no contact with his father during adult life. George was something of a lone wolf with a history of drifting from job to job and from transient involvement to transient involvement. He worked as an unskilled laborer despite considerable intellectual interest and competence and several years of college. He conveyed a sense of militant independence and of aggressiveness in the name of unpopular causes, which held much early appeal for Mary. He could understand and sympathize with that part of Mary which was in revolt against a maternal attachment. George characterized the background of his marriage in this way to the research interviewer: He had never really contemplated marriage, he had never expected to get married, he never exactly proposed.

> I don't know how it happened. We just decided to get married. Maybe we both felt we were beyond our prime and we better marry while anyone would still have us. I had lived by myself ever since I was out of the army, and all my life I've been pretty much of a lone wolf. I enjoy being by myself, being able to do what I want. And when I'm alone, I don't have to worry about hurting anyone.

Thus each partner was in his own fashion strikingly uncommitted to that change of status commemorated by the wedding ceremony. But then this commemoration itself contained a significant reservation: George did not give Mary a wedding ring until six years later, when she was a patient in a mental hospital.

Within two weeks of marriage, George lost his job and, rather than seek work in northern California, moved with his bride to New Jersey and into her mother's apartment. Later they moved to a separate apartment nearby, but Mary continued to see her mother almost daily.

Throughout the early period of the marriage, the Yales quarreled frequently, and there were repeated separations and reunions. Mary moved back and forth, in both physical and emotional space, between mother and husband. The parental and marital families alternately merged and separated. At times the couple lived with her mother; at times they lived by themselves; at times Mary would return alone to the maternal home. She vacillated between being the wife (and later, mother) in one family and being the daughter in the other. Mother and husband stood as opposite poles of attachment, and they, for their part, periodically cooperated to reinstitute the patient's involvement with her mother and alternately acted to rupture this relationship.

Mary felt that the marriage was unfair to her husband because she was not really "serious" about it. She was aware of her competing attachment to her mother. George, for his part, resented his wife's financial and emotional dependence on him. In marriage he consciously experienced a revival of an earlier struggle to avoid attachment to a clinging and possessive woman. When responsibilities were thrust on him or other difficulties loomed, he encouraged his wife to turn to her mother. Mrs. Brown had not been pleased with her daughter's marital choice and ambivalently encouraged separations and efforts at marital reconciliation.

With the birth of a baby in the second year of marriage, separations between the partners became somewhat less frequent, but friction between husband, wife, and mother increased. George resented his mother-in-law's possessiveness toward the baby and pressed at times for moving the family to another city. But he also resented the new financial and emotional burdens he was required to assume, and he became bitterly critical of his wife's "overdependence" on him. Each month he became angry as routine bills arrived for payment, and he had recurrent fantasies of being supported by his wife. Any request by her for emotional support evoked reactions of anger, withdrawal, or active deflection of her dependency toward her mother.

When the child was about a year old, the Yales moved away and lived in a household consisting of only the primary family. After a brief time, however, Mary's mother became ill and was invited to live with them. Her recovery was slow. She became manifestly nervous and irritable. Mary felt threatened by her mother's condition and commented, "I just seemed to lose a lot of confidence in myself when I saw her being ill." The mother, however, remained active during this period. She took over cooking, housework, and child care in the Yale household. To her express surprise and dismay, she found that these activities occasioned frequent, intense arguments with her daughter. Later, reflecting on this, Mrs. Brown said:

> I think my daughter resented me, I feel, because I tried to help her with her work. She didn't seem to want me around. She kept saying she wanted to be on her own and that she didn't have confidence because I was always doing things for her. She even resented me doing the dishes. I just wanted to help out. I didn't have anything to do. I work hard, and I love to work.

During quarrels, Mary would ask her mother to leave her alone and to go away, but she would later attempt to repair the relationship by emphasizing her mother's importance to her. "Mother, you help me more than anyone. I don't know what I would do without you." Periods of intense dependency on her mother alternated with periods of violent repudiation. In the months preceding hospitalization there was a series of transient but frightening ruptures of the mother-daughter relationship. At the same time, George was overtly critical of his mother-in-law and of his wife's attachment to her. He became increasingly absorbed in his work and in a circle of male friends. When his wife complained that she felt left out of his life, he urged her to develop "independent interests." She ambivalently turned to her mother and, on one occasion when that became impossible, to the lady next door.

During the further deterioration of her relationship to her husband and the increased conflict with her mother, Mrs. Yale became absorbed in an intense relationship with the lady next door. This led to the incident which was to stand out in George's memory as the moment when his wife, suddenly as it seemed to him, "broke down." One day Mrs. Brown called George at work, reporting that Mary was extremely upset. He found his wife in bed, weeping and "hysterical." She began to tell him what an awful life the lady next door led and how terrible this woman's marriage was. "Finally it came out that Mary thought this woman was a homosexual." She told him that this woman had made subtle advances toward her, and she stressed that there had not been any physical contact between them. "She made me assure her that I believed her. She clung to me spiritually, emotionally, and physically."

George reassured his wife and transiently accepted her view of the lady next door. He took Mary away from this lady (and from Mrs. Brown) on a brief vacation and agreed with her that she should avoid further contact with the lady. George, in retrospect, told us that "nobody knew she was sick and needed a doctor's care at that time" and that he expected his wife to "snap out of it."

The drama unfolding around Mary, George, and the lady next door thus restated a persistent marital pattern in a new setting. Mary married her husband in a flight from her attachment to her mother and sought in him, among other things, a protector against this attachment. The husband rescued her from this attachment and then relinquished her to it. She asked for his support against the attachment and returned to it persistently. Thus she became involved in an intense relationship with the unhappy lady next door, became frightened, and turned to her husband with this plea: I am in danger from a woman; reassure me of the protection of our relationship. George reassured her, taking her away from the danger. But shortly thereafter George began to convey ambiguous hints that he was seriously considering the possibility of divorce or separation.

Mary's distress continued during the brief vacation and persisted on return. The distress was communicated directly and indirectly to husband and mother and obtruded itself on family life as an insistent call for action. There were homosexual concerns, fears that she was losing her mind, periods of weeping without obvious external cause, and depression to the point of virtual immobilization. Mary began to feel that she needed special help with her problems. Mrs. Brown, upset by her daughter's outbursts of hostility and resentment toward her, believed that her daughter was "not herself" and favored professional assistance, but George thought that the problems his wife was experiencing were minor and transient and did not warrant the expense of seeing a psychiatrist. After limited discussion between husband and wife, it was decided that

Mary should talk with a friend of the family, John Deming, whose legal experience provided some general background in personal counseling. Mr. Deming was George's old friend, one of that small circle of male friends to whom he felt very close and to whom he himself had frequently turned to complain about marital difficulties and to seek advice.

The Yales went together to see Mr. Deming at his home and to consider together the problems of Mrs. Yale. A second meeting was arranged for Mary to see John Deming alone. Later, Mary told her psychiatrist that, every time she criticized her husband, John defended him. In any event, she soon became angry at John and decided to discontinue talks with him.

In this brief encounter with the friend of the family, we observe the beginnings of a process through which Mrs. Yale's distress will come to be defined a psychiatric illness, and special and expert help beyond the family will be solicited. The process is neither simple nor direct, and the consultative relationship to Mr. Deming arises as a kind of compromise.

The friend of the family was, in fact, the close friend of the husband and was experienced by Mary as her husband's ally. This seemed to be, for both partners, one important feature in the inception and termination of the relationship. The compromise, then, reflected the extent to which husband and wife latently conceived of her disturbance and its resolution as intimately connected to their marriage and its future. The choice of Mr. Deming, as Mary soon discovered, inherently limited the possibilities of resolution. The choice of Mr. Deming was also a compromise between conflicting definitions of how seriously Mary's communications of distress were to be taken. At the level of the marital dialogue, Mary's expressed need for help, like her earlier quest for reassurance after the incident with the lady next door, was experienced as a claim on her husband. Mr. Yale questioned the claim and anticipated that his wife would "snap out of it." It is true that the family, already in debt and living marginally, could not readily afford psychiatric treatment. But the realities of the wife's distress and of the family's limited financial resources repeated, in intense form and in an "insoluble" situation, the pattern of the husband's grudging, resentful, and limited acceptance of the provider role *and* the question both had shared throughout their marriage—the validity of Mary's emotional and material demands on her husband.

After the termination of her talks with John Deming, Mary asked her physician for psychiatric referral. She was immediately seen by a psychiatrist who accepted her for outpatient treatment and recommended that she begin on a twice-a-week basis. Mary told him she did not feel she could afford more than one appointment a week and expressed guilt about spending any money at all on herself.

Shortly after treatment began, Mrs. Brown telephoned the psychiatrist to express concern about her daughter's condition, to solicit information, and specifically to ask the doctor's opinion as to whether she (Mrs. Brown) ought to move away, as her daughter sometimes demanded, or remain nearby to render assistance. This question was clearly a test of whether the doctor was an ally or a foe. The psychiatrist stressed the confidentiality of the treatment situation, indicated that he would inform the daughter of the mother's call, would not discuss the treatment, and offered no advice about what Mrs. Brown should do. Mrs. Brown felt hurt and angry and later commented to the research interviewer, "I'm the kind of mother who worries about her children and whose whole life centers around my children."

A few weeks later, Mrs. Brown encouraged her daughter to get away from all her worries by going on an extended vacation with her. Mary accepted. This vacation lasted about a month, interrupted the treatment, detached the daughter from her incipient tie to the physician, and re-established the pattern of mother-daughter interdependency with the husband at the periphery of involvement. George continued to doubt that his wife's situation was serious enough to warrant treatment and told her so, openly deplored the expense, and seemed concerned lest treatment lead to new demands on him for closer involvement with his wife. He was ambivalently and covertly considering seeking a separation.

Mary's own difficulties in sustaining a therapeutic relation-

ship were closely linked to cross pressures in this triad. She felt
guilty about spending her husband's money on herself (for treatment) and about pressing any overt claims on him. She also experienced the treatment as an act of disloyalty toward her mother
and as a threat to that relationship. When her mother suggested
the vacation which would interrupt the treatment, Mrs. Yale
consented. The psychiatrist's impressions of the case, summarized
after Mrs. Yale's hospitalization, provides a supplementary perspective on the processes we have described:

> As therapy progressed, it became clear to me that
> Mrs. Yale was in a tightly interlocked symbiotic rela-
> tionship with her mother. It was as though literally her
> mother were part of her and that to ask her mother
> to leave was to cut off part of her own body. Mrs.
> Yale felt in the impossible situation of having to be-
> long simultaneously to both her mother and husband
> and considered that there was something defective and
> "crazy" about her because she couldn't.

In the period preceding hospitalization Mary Yale was preoccupied with a series of questions about herself. Was she becoming homosexual? Was she going insane? How could she go
on? Simultaneously, she was involved in a network of intimate
relations in which an echoing set of questions was raised. Was
she going to leave her husband and live with her mother? Was
she going to stay with her husband and ask her mother to leave?
How could she leave these decisions unmade? The reality of her
situation corresponded to this experience of a forced and drastic
choice. Her husband had become overtly critical of her involvement with her mother and at times demanded that she choose
between them; at other times he spoke to her of separation or
divorce. Her mother pressed claims competitive to the marriage
through illness, through participation in the management of the
household, and through criticisms of the spouse.

It was in this context that the psychotic episode occurred as
a restatement, in intensified form and under altered conditions,
of a chronic struggle. These altered conditions seemed to have

the significance of blocking her movement between the parental and marital families, between mother and husband. Both alternatives were desperately affirmed and repudiated in the period preceding hospitalization, but in time she came to feel alienated from *both* mother and husband and driven toward increasing psychic withdrawal, which did not resolve her conflicts or remove her from the triad. She herself finally pushed for physical removal by requesting hospitalization.

CRISES OF SEPARATION

The case of Mary Yale illustrates one type of conflict mobilized in study group women by movement into adult roles in marital families of their own. The transitional crises in five additional cases (Karr, Price, Low, Arlen, Thorne) are sufficiently similar to warrant consideration of the six cases as a group. These women all foundered on the task of separation, especially from ties to the mother: leaving home, detaching themselves from the claims of the maternal attachment, establishing some sense of self apart from childhood roles in the parental family.

The early developmental history of these women, which forms the inner basis for later transitions, is not known to us in detail. We conceive here that normal progression from an infantile symbiotic phase, in which the person is undifferentiated from the maternal matrix, to a mature stage of relative independence moves through a series of object relations. The growing infant differentiates himself from his mother, establishes ego boundaries, and seeks out new objects—father, friends, and others. The orderly establishment of object relations requires and develops the capacity for commitment to important new relationships and the ability to separate from old ones. *These separations require especially a change in the character of the maternal relationship from an exclusive involvement to a new integration that will allow for other object relations.* Movement along this developmental track forms the inner basis for later mature heterosexual relationships, including marriage, and for the assumption of the relationship of parent to children. We infer, but cannot demonstrate from *early* material, that the women described here were unable to firmly accomplish the differentiation from the mother-child symbiotic identification and the establishment of the father as the preferred love object. This early developmental failure made them vulnerable to the crises they experienced in attempting the transitions of marriage and parenthood.

From the data at our disposal, we are able to establish that these women remained more-or-less encapsulated in the parental family prior to marriage and had established few stable involvements in extrafamilial roles. In some cases, such as that of Mrs. Yale, the young woman had remained attached to her mother well into young adulthood in a type of reciprocated symbiotic involvement similar to that described by Lewis B. Hill, Murray Bowen, Theodore Lidz, David Limentani, and others.[5] In such cases, the mother had been unable to tolerate separation from her daughter, had experienced the latter's growth and independence as a threat, and had undermined the daughter's attempts to encounter and master increasing segments of reality. These young women entered marriage in a desperate flight from the claims of this attachment but soon turned toward their mothers to reestablish a symbiotic relationship. In the contemporary marital family, the mother shared the daughter's complaints about the husband, covertly or even overtly encouraged withdrawal from marriage, and offered herself as a continuing alternative to marital involvement. At the same time, the mothers more-or-less subtly defined marital troubles as personal failures of their daughters and berated separation or divorce. This pattern has been illustrated by the case of Mrs. Yale but may be briefly supplemented by another brief case excerpt.

[5] Lewis B. Hill, *Psychotherapeutic Intervention in Schizophrenia* (Chicago: University of Chicago Press, 1955); Murray Bowen, "A Family Concept of Schizophrenia," in Jackson, *op. cit.*, pp. 346–372; Lidz and Fleck, *op. cit.*; Limentani, *op. cit.*; George C. Lyketsos, "On the Formation of Mother-Daughter Symbiotic Relationship Patterns in Schizophrenia," *Psychiatry*, XXII (1959), 161–166; Helm Stierlin, "The Adaptation to the 'Stronger' Person's Reality: Some Aspects of the Symbiotic Relationship of the Schizophrenic," *Psychiatry*, XXII (1959), 143–152.

Mrs. Low, a shy and inhibited twenty-six-year-old woman, met a stranger on a train while en route home to visit her mother and became engaged to marry him. In spite of her mother's disapproval, the marriage took place, and Mrs. Low moved away with her husband. Shortly afterward, she began to question her love for her husband and abruptly returned to her mother and accepted employment in the place where her mother had worked. Later her husband joined her, and the marital relationship resumed. For long periods Mrs. Low's mother lived with them and assumed most of the responsibility for housework and child care. Mrs. Low turned to her for advice and emotional support. At other times the couple lived in an independent household and more-or-less consciously attempted to establish a closer marital relationship.

The active role of the mothers in sustaining the transition difficulties experienced by these women may be further underlined by summarizing the results of an analysis of Eve Low's mother's expressed attitudes toward Eve's husband. In the course of two lengthy recorded interviews, Eve's mother said that Chester Low was uncommunicative, stubborn—"You can't talk to him"—promiscuous, and a poor provider. He did not take his job seriously; he did not know the value of money and ran up bills he could not pay. He subjected his wife and children to poor living conditions. He was a misfit who could not do anything really well. He was dependent, relying heavily on the help given him by his own as well as Eve's mother. He was not good enough for Eve—he was her intellectual and educational inferior. Even his own relatives did not care for him. Up to a point, Eve shared her mother's attitudes toward her husband but, as in the case of Mrs. Yale and the other separation cases, harbored alternative hopes that the husband would prove a protector against or a substitute for the maternal tie.

In three cases (Price, Arlen, and Thorne) the mothers did not appear to have attempted to maintain a persisting, exclusive

involvement with their daughters. If their mothers did not reveal
dependency on involvement with their daughters, their daughters
nonetheless revealed a continued dependent involvement with
their mothers or maternal substitutes. They remained passive, personally helpless, and encapsulated in the parental family. These
women seemed to drift, with increasing age and the shifting requirements of social reality, into marriage and motherhood. Facing
the demands of adult life, they attempted to establish a symbiotic
integration, at first with their husbands and eventually with their
mothers.

> During the first year of her marriage, Cora Thorne
> became "scared to death of being alone." She would
> go to her mother's house, a few blocks away, until her
> husband returned from work. Peter Thorne later char-
> acterized his wife throughout their marriage as "hav-
> ing an overdeveloped imagination," "afraid of being
> alone," and "needing the company of her mother."
> When she did not walk over to her mother's, she
> would talk to her on the phone "for hours." Even-
> tually, Peter Thorne had a phone put into the kitchen
> for Cora's use so that her "yak-yak" would not inter-
> rupt his television-watching.

The husband in all six cases assumed strategic significance
as the agent through which a psychic movement away from the
mother was to be accomplished or sustained. In some instances
the husband seemed to be a differentiated love object, and the
wife struggled with the choice between love for a woman and love
for a man. An earlier transition which miscarried—the shift of
love object from the mother to the father—was refought on a
new battleground. In other instances, the husband seemed to
stand as a maternal substitute, the object of primarily symbiotic
rather than Oedipal longings.

A distinctive characteristic of the six cases is that, at earlier
crossroads of ego development and again in marital life, various
impulses and strivings had called for the integration of a new
relationship and the renunciation of symbiotic ties. The daugh-

ters had met this call with feelings of panic, emptiness, and incompleteness. They had responded to these feelings by an attempt to create or re-establish a symbiotic tie.

These women encountered a critical struggle in early adult life when their own strivings, defenses against infantile object ties, and the requirements of reality pressed by the wider society led them to seek or to accept movement out of symbiotic bonds. This movement toward differentiation and independence initiated panic and an attempt to restore symbiotic relationships. This retreat, in turn, activated struggles against anxieties about fusion. The polarities of separation and fusion dominated marital life and were often expressed in physical as well as in psychic space. For example, some of these women repeatedly moved back and forth between the maternal and marital homes.

None of these women experienced a psychotic episode in immediate conjunction with leaving home and marriage. The vicissitudes of their crises were played out in contemporary family contexts which mitigated or intensified their personal conflicts. We must distinguish a period of precarious equilibrium, in which severe conflict was present but somehow contained, from a later period, when defensive and adaptive efforts failed. This distinction will require us to consider the type of role established in these families for the wives and the ways in which this role became untenable. It is evident from the Yale case that the organization of marital family life is not determined by the wife's requirements and conflicts alone, but by interlocking anxieties, conflicts, and conditions of intimacy in a family group. It is to this description and analysis that we now turn.

3

Family Processes

Crises of Separation

In the history of the Yale marriage, there was a recurrent sequence.[1] The primary marital family unit would establish itself in an independent household and function for a time as an isolated nuclear family. This arrangement would eventually prove unstable and would yield to one of two alternatives—either the wife would leave her husband and move in with her mother or her mother would be invited to move in with the marital family. After a time these arrangements would collapse, and the wife would return to her husband, or the mother would exclude herself or be excluded from the marital household, and the marital family would again be established as an independent unit. The repeated transformations are summarized in the following diagram.

The "stable instability" which characterized this marital family resulted from the interlocking stresses of each arrangement for all three participants. The primary marital family unit moved

[1] This chapter is based in part on an earlier article, "Schizophrenia and the Marital Family: Accommodations to Symbiosis," and portions have been reprinted with the permission of *Family Process*, I, No. 2 (1962), 304–318.

Stage 1	Stage 2	Stage 3	Stage 4	Stage 5
	Wife returns to mother	→ Wife returns to husband		
Establishment of primary marital family unit			Same as Stage 2	→ Same as Stage 3
	Mother lives with marital partners (or vice-versa)	→ Mother leaves marital partners (or vice-versa)		

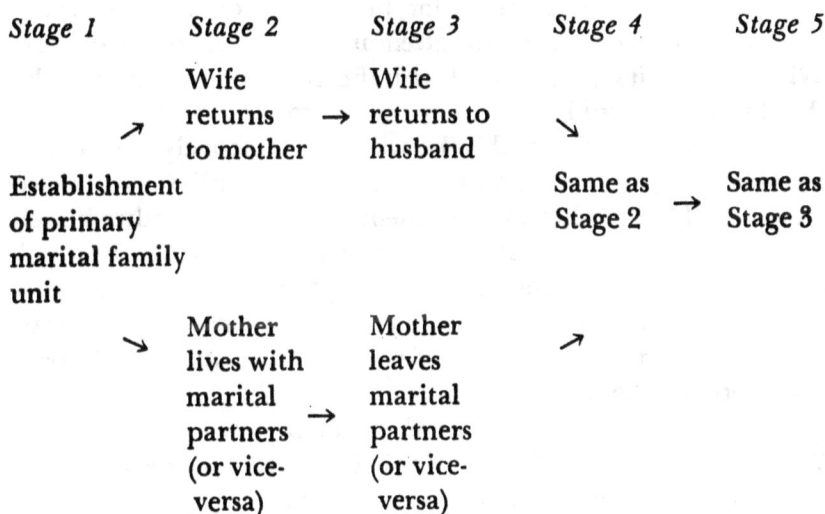

toward disruption in response to various pressures. The husband tended to withdraw from the demands of marital intimacy and responsibility and to foster his wife's dependency on her mother. The prototype of this recurring situation was Mr. Yale's loss of a job as an unskilled laborer within two weeks of marriage and the decision to leave this area with his new bride and move in with his mother-in-law. The mother repeatedly made herself available to Mrs. Yale as an alternative love object and openly pressed claims competitive to the husband. Mrs. Yale was invariably responsive to her mother's claims and often initiated these claims herself through complaints about her marriage, through illness, and through appeals for involvement. In any given instance, one or another of these factors seemed dominant, but it was usually obvious that the husband, the wife, and the mother were effectively collaborating in turning the young woman toward her mother.

Separations of the marital partners were, however, equally unstable. The wife could not tolerate living alone and experienced grave threats to her identity when living with her mother. Mr. Yale also seemed unable to tolerate a definitive breach of the marital relationship and would eventually make overtures toward its resumption. The mother, for her part, would ambivalently encourage her daughter to attempt a marital reconciliation. When the marital family lived with the mother in one household, the husband would eventually move to breach the mother-daughter attachment. In this, he was usually actively encouraged by Mrs. Yale, notwithstanding that she had earlier encouraged and invited her mother's involvement. Finally, the mother herself sometimes moved to disassemble the merged family unit, although in the process she usually attempted to take her daughter with her. Thus, the pattern of cyclic involvement which characterized the marital history reflected shifting stakes and coalitions between the three persons.

What were the effects of these family processes on Mrs. Yale's personal crisis of separation? The patterned instability of the family provided continuing support for her own vacillation between love objects, between families, and between childhood and adult roles. She maintained mother and husband, parental and marital families, as opposite poles of attachment. She used each alternative as a defense against the anxieties mobilized by the other, and she avoided firm integration into either. The price of this accommodation was prolongation of the transitional crisis. Further, the conflict was kept alive as an almost day-to-day crisis by the continuing availability of and pressure for whichever arrangement was not at that moment in force. When changing circumstances reduced her freedom of maneuver and implicitly pressed for a firm choice, the dilemma she experienced was expressed in schizophrenic disorganization.

MERGER: THE TRIGENERATIONAL FAMILY

In each of the separation cases, the members of the marital family attempted to establish a separate, relatively self-contained nuclear family. In each case, the attempt was unsuccessful. Over time, alternative organizations of family life characterized by a gross blurring of boundaries between generations were established. In the Yale case, no alternative organization proved stable, and repeated movement between alternatives characterized the family history. With some differences in the interlocking needs of the participants, however, the family could move toward a relatively stable establishment of one of the alternative organizations.

Wanda Karr

The Karr family provides an illustration of a trend toward a relatively stable organization which may be called merger. In the merged family, the marital and parental families tend to be condensed into an enduring trigenerational unit, with the maternal figure from the parental family assuming *de facto* emotional and authoritative leadership. This places the wife directly in a regressive symbiotic maternal relationship in the context of new and conflicting demands posed by the marital family.

Until marriage at the age of twenty-five, Wanda Karr's relationship with her mother had been characterized by protectiveness and interference on the mother's side and by dependence, awe, and subdued resentment on Wanda's part. She had established no enduring interests or relationships outside of her immediate family. After a brief courtship, she married "the only boy [she] ever really went with." Her mother explicitly opposed the marriage. Although Wanda felt ill on her wedding day, she went through with the ceremony and moved out of the parental home for the first time.

The separation did not last. After living briefly in a small, furnished apartment, the Karrs acceded to an invitation from the mother to accept financial assistance for the purchase of a house. They moved next door to the mother. With this move, daughter and mother began to see each other daily. The Karrs began to eat many meals at the mother's house. At the mother's suggestion, they sold their automobile and borrowed hers, thus requiring them to ask for permission on the infrequent occasions when they wanted to go out. The mother routinely questioned their requests and often refused permission. They did not install a telephone and could only phone or be phoned at the mother's residence. Wanda relied on her mother extensively for assistance with furnishing and housework, and the mother actively offered assistance. Richard Karr, Wanda's husband, turned to the mother for advice about insurance, physicians, and his job. In brief, the Karrs made few decisions without consulting the mother; when they did, the mother would question the appropriateness of their choices. In time, the term "we" as used by the Karrs or the mother came to refer to the Karr family plus Wanda's family of origin.

The presence of the first child intensified the need of wife, husband, and mother for these patterns of interdependency, while increasing conflicts about them. Wanda began to express irritation to her husband about the mother's usurpation of her relationship with her first child. The child called both women "Mama," both houses "home," and turned to her grandmother when faced with her parents' strictures. According to the Karrs, the mother "always took the child's side." Richard was also irritated by this development, but his wife's growing antagonism toward her mother made him feel, as he said, "in the middle." That his wife would not for long countenance overt expressions of antagonism toward her mother contributed to this feeling.

During her second pregnancy, even more than during her first, Wanda felt "nervous" and tired. Her mother and husband frequently told her she looked ill and would urge her to be passive. Wanda would lie down and then have trouble arising. But along with this regression from caring for to being cared for, Wanda had an opposing motive. She had not nursed her first child and had deferred much of the responsibility for feeding to her mother and husband. She planned, however, to nurse the second child. She began to do so, successfully, in the hospital. When she came home, however, her tension increased. She could neither nurse nor relinquish the striving to do so, and her breasts began to swell and ache. Her mother came to stay with her and to apply home remedies to her painful breasts. Wanda's mother saw the problem as "drying up" the milk. Wanda, on the other hand, saw the problem as increasing the milk flow so that she might continue to nurse. To this end, she began to drink large quantities of water. A sedative, prescribed by the family physician over the telephone, was interpreted by mother and daughter as intended to accomplish these conflicting objectives. During this interval Wanda's mother moved into Wanda's house.

This was the setting of the psychotic episode. Wanda's efforts to nurse her child dissolved in failure, her breasts became a source of unbearable pain, and the striving to mother succumbed to the experience of being mothered. She became slovenly and withdrawn. She began to "preach" about her mother's "cruelty" and her husband's "infidelity." She asked her mother to play dolls with her, placing a doll on the bed between her mother and herself. A psychiatrist was contacted, and Wanda became a mental patient two weeks after delivery.

The merged family organization afforded a precarious solution to the functional requirements of marital life and to the interlocking requirements and conflicts of the participants. When the wife tended to withdraw from critical family functions, her mother tended to take over. On the other side of this complicated reciprocity, when the mother pressed to take over marital family functions, the wife withdrew. Thus for a time the marital family was able to continue.

The merged family accommodated Wanda Karr's sense of inadequacy and her involvement with an enveloping mother. At the same time, she did not have to entirely relinquish her precarious ties to strivings as a wife and mother. Self-reproaches as well as those of others were deflected for a time by a shared family ideology that Wanda was "weak" and "sickly," that the extrafamily world was cold and dangerous, and that the mother was a benevolent helper and protective shield. This shared ideology supported Wanda's personal reliance on defensive strategies of regression and projection. Further, the family pattern served to compensate the mother's sense of loss at her daughter's marriage, and it preserved her claims to the latter's deference and submission. The mother repeatedly invited her daughter to regress. The daughter not only acceded to these invitations, but often prompted them by withdrawal from responsibilities, by physical illness, and by the demands of helplessness.

The potentially competing claims of the marital family were muted for a time by the husband's readiness to participate in these arrangements. In this, he received direct encouragement from his wife's insistence on the benevolence of her mother, her mother's need for her, and her need for her mother. Richard Karr himself preferred almost anything to overt disputes, and this contributed to his readiness to passively encourage the merger. Further, the arrangement relieved him of marital responsibilities, and it accommodated his own requirements for a dependent relationship with a maternal person. Once the arrangement was established, Mr. Karr tended to play down and to try to undo the growing tension between Wanda and her mother, in effect supporting his wife's dependency on her mother and tying all three more closely together.

Shirley Arlen

A similar solution was attempted in the Arlen family. In this instance, it was the husband's mother who initially fostered and accommodated the wife's withdrawal, driven in part by her urgent desire not to lose her son.

Shirley Arlen was pregnant at the time of her marriage and from the beginning felt overwhelmed by the responsibilities she had assumed. She could not spend money because it did not really belong to her. She had never taken responsibility for shopping for groceries and clothes and could not do so now. She did not feel able to decide what to cook and felt uneasy in preparing the meals. Even routine housework seemed to her more than she could manage. About one month before the birth of the first child, the Arlens moved in with James's parents. The care of the first-born was rather rapidly and exclusively appropriated by James Arlen's mother, who treated the child as though it were her own. Although she now wished to assume responsibility herself, Shirley was afraid to protest. The situation grew worse for her—she began to retire for the evening by eight o'clock and found it increasingly difficult to assume any adult role in the household.

A few months after the birth of her first child, Shirley suspected that she was again pregnant. The same month, she and James moved to a rented house of their own. Shirley was very eager to move out of her mother-in-law's house, but once again the responsibilities proved frightening. She would put off household chores. James would take over, and she would then feel increasingly anxious and guilty. She became lax in caring for the child, leaving him in bed for most of the day and rarely playing with him.

Shortly before the birth of the second child, James's parents invited the Arlens to move in with them again. They refused the invitation. But after the birth, Shirley spent much time in bed. She did not cook dinner, and her husband had to prepare his own meals. He did the house-cleaning and brought the laundry to his parents' home. Shirley would feel ill each morning and would ask him to take the older child to his mother's for the day. A little later, Shirley and her husband consulted a psychiatrist at the recommendation of her physician. The psychiatrist saw her weekly, and urged the husband to come in, too. The husband declined to do so. During this period, Shirley's own mother agreed to come over during the days to provide help. When Shirley's father became ill and her mother was unable to come, Shirley asked her mother to take the newborn child with her and care for him. This was done. A few days later Shirley, too, moved to her mother's house. That evening James visited her and told her that, if she was sick, he could not afford to maintain their home. He moved, then, into his mother's house with the older child. A week later Shirley told her mother that she had decided to go to the hospital because she feared she was losing her mind and might harm someone. Her mother tried to discourage her, but Shirley took a cab to the hospital that morning.

CONVERSION: HUSBAND-WIFE SYMBIOSIS

We observed one other distinguishable variation in types of family solutions to the crisis of separation. The Price family at various stages of their marital history attempted arrangements already familiar to us from the preceding cases. Over time, however, the pattern of accommodation moved toward that of an isolated nuclear family which *itself* came to serve the wife as a substitute for the parental family. We may term this a conversion of the marital family into a quasi-parental family in which a regressive symbiotic relationship is created.

At the age of twenty, Rose Price married a man in his thirties who viewed her as helpless, dependent, and in need of care. His solicitude conveyed to her a desire to help her out of an unhappy family situation. The Prices lived near her family in the first years of marriage, and Rose often turned to her mother and older sisters during "spells" of acute discomfort. These periods were characterized by Mrs. Price's loss of interest in housework and child care, by multiple and vague physical complaints, and by an expressed need to have someone with her at all times. If her female relatives were not available, Rose would relentlessly cling to her husband, demanding to accompany him to work and elsewhere. She would, when permitted, sit at his side during a full work shift. The initial "spell" occurred during Mrs. Price's first pregnancy.

After several years of marriage, William Price insisted on moving to California. Rose unsuccessfully opposed moving on the grounds that at home her family assisted her when she needed help. After the move, Rose's "spells" were punctuated by trips home during which she was cared for by her family. Later, when William's opposition prevented a return to the parental home, Rose began to hear her parents talking to her and telling her to take care of herself. She believed that, when she was sick, her parents were able to directly communicate their concern to her.

As the result of a complicated reciprocity between the spouses, William Price assumed more and more of his wife's household functions, becoming both father and mother to the children, as well as caretaker for his wife. Rose withdrew into helplessness and inactivity. William Price criticized his wife's performances of marital roles, complaining that the house was never clean, the dinner was never good, and child care never adequate. Despite such complaints, he failed to repair a broken kitchen sink, and Rose had to wash dishes in the bathroom. He made no effort to repair their badly deteriorated house or to move. He viewed his wife's wishes to visit with neighbors or relatives as "restlessness," refused her the use of the family automobile, and would not install a telephone. When Rose found part-time work and companionship in a neighbor's home, William induced her to quit.

Rose Price lived in isolation from neighbors, had no friends, seldom saw relatives, and had little contact outside of her marital family. Within it, she was subject to constant criticism and depreciation. William Price encouraged his sons to ignore their mother's requests and formed a particularly close alliance with the youngest son, Mike, four years old. He was, in the language of both parents, "Daddy's boy." He called his father "Honey," and he was not reprimanded by Mr. Price when he called his mother "crazy." At Mr. Price's invitation, the boy slept between his father and mother. In front of the boy William Price accused his wife of hating her son and of wishing to harm him. He placed himself in the role of his son's protector against an unnatural mother. The son was, in a real sense, his mother's rival for Mr. Price's maternal affections.

The degree to which Rose Price was removed from any effective mother role in the family is clear in this incident observed by the research interviewer.

> Mike walked into the room, and Rose said, "I bought a new fishing pole." "You mean Daddy did," Mike responded. Rose didn't comment. Mike walked over to the corner of the room and picked up the fishing pole. He started fussing with it and then hollered out angrily, "Why, you got this tangled up! Come here and fix it!" Rose looked over and said, "Bring it over, sweetheart." There was complete silence, and he didn't bring it over. Finally she got up and went over to Mike and the pole. He again yelled at her to fix it, adding "Don't hit me, or I'll hit you!" Rose attempted to untangle the fishing line, and Mike scolded her angrily. She eventually got it untangled and then leaned the pole against the wall. Mike told her sternly not to put it there but to put it away in the bedroom. He then went out of the house, and Rose called after him, "Don't run off too far. Mommy will be out with you shortly."

This was the background of Rose Price's further disorganization. Her dependence on female relatives was interrupted, only to be transferred to her husband. William Price supported this transfer, as well as the need for it, by isolating her from others and by participating in her helplessness in the marital family. At the time of hospitalization, Mrs. Price was constantly preoccupied with fears that her youngest son would be harmed. And she insisted that she was pregnant, although this was not confirmed by medical examination. In this function, at least, she could not be replaced by her husband or youngest son.

This family organization also afforded a partial and precarious solution to the functional requirements of marital family life and to the interlocking requirements and conflicts of the participants. When the wife withdrew from role performance, the husband took over her functions, and from the wife's perspective the family took on many of the characteristics of a parental family. This process was a reciprocal one, for this husband moved to usurp his wife's roles even as she moved to withdraw into helplessness, dependence, and inactivity. The marital family continued, but at the cost of institutionalizing the wife's helplessness through fixed patterns of interaction and without removing the wife from continuing inner and outer demands and reproaches about her performance as wife and mother.

The most obvious reason for this family's shift from a merger toward a conversion was the husband's eventual unwillingness to tolerate his wife's dependence on her female relatives. This factor may also have been connected to special features of his own involvement in the marital symbiosis. His wife's helplessness and dependency had constituted part of her initial appeal for him and served to emphasize his own strength, activity, and masculinity. Their relationship resembled the pairing of "inadequate" and "overadequate" family members described by Murray Bowen and his co-workers.[2] At the same time, the family situation provided a cover under which Mr. Price could and did assume a maternal role and form very close, sexually colored attachments

2 Bowen, *op. cit.*

with his sons. In time his sons, especially the youngest, displaced his wife more and more as objects of involvement, and she became increasingly superfluous to his own adaptive patterns.

Rose Price's symbiotic needs were partially accommodated by the marital arrangements—both the earlier one, which bordered on merger, and the later one, conversion. The marital relationship created a role for her which simultaneously sustained her helplessness and the claims of her marital roles. As her husband withdrew from her and failed to provide either symbiotic support or encouragement for tentative endeavors to assume marital and maternal responsibilities, she became increasingly autistic. The marital relationship became less one of reciprocated symbiosis than of reciprocated withdrawal. This point warrants further comment. Our impression from the six separation cases is that conversion of the marital family into a pseudo-parental family cannot persist for very long, that husbands cannot or will not reciprocate wives' infantile symbiotic needs over any sustained period, and that the direction of change must thus move toward triadic arrangements with a participating mother figure or toward a pattern of reciprocated withdrawal, as in the Price case.

PERSONAL AND FAMILY SEPARATION CRISES

The personal task and crisis of separation for these women was at the same time a task and crisis of the marital family unit. At this level of analysis, the crisis of separation refers to the separation of families, parental from marital, and the separation of roles in the new family, especially those of children from those of parents. In these marital families, the attempt to establish and preserve adequate boundaries between generations failed, and alternative organizations of family life were established. The failures, and the family patterns which thereupon evolved, resulted from interlocking conflicts of a network of intimates as they confronted their respective tasks of adaptation to the changing reciprocities required by the marriage and the birth of children.

The three patterns described had this similarity: they af-

forded the wives an ongoing or intermittent symbiotic relationship while preserving their partial involvement in the demands
and strivings associated with participation in the marital family.
This ambiguous role became a routine feature of family life; that
is, the wives' conflicts were institutionalized in social structures
which pressed competing claims. This role served on the one
hand to mute the full force of anxieties posed by the demands
of marriage and motherhood and on the other hand to moderate
the regressive anxieties mobilized by involvement in a symbiotic
relationship. The precarious personal equilibrium thus established depended on family structures which would continue to
afford the wives the possibility of movement between regressive
and progressive strivings, allowing the anxieties associated with
one alternative to be played off against the anxieties associated
with the other. When these family structures were altered by
inner or outer forces which blocked one or the other possibility,
the wives experienced an intolerable dilemma and suffered
schizophrenic disorganization. The observed conditions which
disrupted the prior equilibrium included the husband's withdrawal, the husband's pressure for the wife to definitively
"choose" between himself and her mother, or the simultaneous
pressures to mother her child and to be mothered herself. This
model of precipitation is unquestionably gross and incomplete,
but it represents an attempt to account for the observation that
mechanisms of ego defense, patterns of interpersonal relations,
and supportive family structures failed hand in hand.

The family organization which we have designated conversion differs from the other variants in the absence of a continuing triad. We suggest that marital family cannot maintain
this type of organization, especially when children are present.
In any event, the precipitational stream differed somewhat in this
instance. The reciprocated symbiosis between the marital partners
changed over time toward reciprocated (mutual) withdrawal, and
the wife, cut off from any meaningful participation in external
reality, became increasingly autistic and gradually deteriorated.

The triadic arrangements present in both of the other forms
of family organization may bear some relation to observations

made by others of persisting mother-child symbioses in the parental family. Intensive studies of parental families have suggested that the father plays a crucial role, often by omission, in the inability of mother and child to relinquish their symbiotic involvement. The absent, withdrawn, or covertly compliant father leads the mother to form an indissoluble libidinal tie to her child and affords the child no sanction, support, or steppingstone for movement beyond the maternal tie. In the marital families we have described, the husband is cast in the role of the alternative to the maternal tie and plays a strategic part—by passive withdrawal and active compliance—in sustaining symbiotic ties to the mother. This observation supports a more general thesis that pathological symbiotic relationships can be maintained only if the participants remain insulated from the ordinary play of expectations, opportunities, and gratifications pressed by the outer world. The father is the typical first representative of the outer world for the mother and her new child, pressing competing claims and incentives on both. In the much later developmental process we have depicted, the husband is heir to a special version of this role.

4

Kate White

Crises of Identification

We have been able to identify a second type of crisis mobilized by movement into adult roles in marital families.[1] In the preceding cases, marital life posed the requirement of differentiation from the mother or from a type of dependence and symbiotic identification modeled after the earliest mother-child relationship. In the group of four cases now to be considered, the crisis was not mobilized by a threat *of* differentiation, but by a threat *to* a previously established differentiation of self from maternal identifications. For these women, the crucial threat posed by participation in the marital family was the revival of certain identifications linked to their mothers.

In the past, in conjunction with various critical events, these women had instituted defenses against this threatening constellation of identifications. The split-off constellation was

---

[1] Portions of this chapter have been published in, and are reprinted with permission from, the *Bulletin of the Menninger Clinic*, (1961), pp. 296–306. Copyright 1961 by the Menninger Foundation. Other portions of this chapter have previously been published in *The Journal of Nervous and Mental Disease*, CXXXIII, No. 5 (1961), 423–429. Portions are reprinted by permission of the editor and publisher. Copyright © 1961, The Williams & Wilkins Co.

revived by transitions of adult life which placed the woman in a marital situation resembling that of her mother. The anniversary reactions documented by Hilgard and her associates, which sensitized us to this phenomenon in our materials, provide dramatic ilustrations of cases for whom marital life revived threatening identifications.[2] Greenson has also presented cases in which the struggle against identifications was essential to the integrity of the "adult" self.[3] Benedek's view that children at each critical stage of their development revive in the parent his related developmental conflicts is also directly relevant to our understanding of these crises.[4]

This type of transitional crisis is illustrated by the case of Kate White. Her crisis is considered from three perspectives in turn. The first perspective concerns the vicissitudes of developmental stages in early childhood which form the inner basis for mastering the progressive demands of adult life. The second concerns the nature of the developmental tasks posed by marital life which were strategically linked to her earlier history. The final and most distinctive perspective concerns contemporary family patterns in their relation to her personal crisis. Each perspective contributes to understanding, and is interwoven in, the single but complex reality of her episode.

EARLY DEVELOPMENT
AND THE CRISIS OF IDENTIFICATION

Kate White was the second of two daughters. She had been a difficult pregnancy and birth for her mother, who was confined to bed for a month *post partum*. In the first year of life, Kate had

2 Josephine R. Hilgard, "Anniversary Reactions in Parents Precipitated by Children," *Psychiatry*, XVI (1953), 73–80; Josephine R. Hilgard and Martha F. Newman, "Anniversaries in Mental Illness," *Psychiatry*, XXII (1959), 113–121; Josephine R. Hilgard and Fern Fisk, "Disruption of Adult Ego Identity as Related to Childhood Loss of a Mother Through Hospitalization for Psychosis," *The Journal of Nervous and Mental Disease*, CXXXI (1960), 47–57; Hilgard, Newman, and Fisk, "Strength of Adult Ego Following Childhood Bereavement." *American Journal of Orthopsychiatry*, XXX (1960), 788–798.

3 Ralph R. Greenson, "The Struggle Against Identification," *Journal of the American Psychoanalytic Association*, II (1954), 200–217.

4 Therese F. Benedek, "Parenthood as a Developmental Phase," *Journal of the American Psychoanalytic Association*, VII (1959), 389–417.

two serious illnesses necessitating considerable special care. These experiences, frequently recounted by her mother, contributed to a later sense of fragility and lack of appeal. Her sister's docile obedience contrasted with her own active rebelliousness, and her sister was quite clearly her mother's favorite, while she became her father's.

Father replaced mother in Kate's life at a very early date. His marriage was unhappy, and his young daughter became the focus of his life in the family. He provided the love and affection she felt lacking from her mother, and Kate was pleased by her pre-eminent place in his life. This attachment became prepossessing and complemented and supported the turning from her mother.

Kate's positive identifications were with her father rather than her mother, and her sexual orientation became significantly masculine rather than feminine. This development was reinforced by the unrewarding picture of female life portrayed by her mother. The father had been carrying on a long-standing affair with his secretary, but the parents had decided to remain together, ostensibly for the sake of the children. The affair was known to the mother, but initially kept from the children, who, however, had reason to suspect it. When Kate was eight or nine years old, her mother openly confronted the daughters with their father's infidelity and made a direct bid for their sympathy and allegiance. Womanhood was characterized as a precarious and suffering position, faced with the constant threat of desertion and victimization, an estate with little appeal or opportunity for satisfaction.

The father's extramarital affair, combined with his already strong attachment for his younger daughter, served to intensify the erotic implications of their relationship. During latency Kate had become a tomboy who identified with father's active, independent, and rebellious attitude toward life. She took his professional career and philosophy of life as models for her own. However, at adolescence, when her relationship to boys became an issue, her father's jealous possessiveness became a difficult problem. Even in young adulthood, Kate's father intervened forcefully to disrupt a budding relation she had excitedly and fearfully begun to form with an older married man. Kate was chagrined by her father's arbitrary and authoritarian intervention in this illicit relationship, but she was also pleased by the demonstration of his possessive love and interest in her. Kate's attachment to her father thus provided a substitute for the maternal attachment but reinforced her negative response to her mother and to womanhood; provided a masculine model, complicated by infidelity, for identification; and established a gratifying erotic tie difficult to relinquish in favor of later potential love objects.

At the time of her psychotic episode, Mrs. White's marital family repeated many significant features of her parental family. The marital family consisted of two daughters, a father away from home much of the time, and a mother who felt martyred. Some of Kate White's symptoms reflected a reliving of distressing aspects of her own childhood through identifications with her children. She felt her daughters had come into possession of some terrible information which they had not been meant to know and that this unspecified knowledge would cause them great harm. The children seemed to be giving her "signs" that indicated she should leave her husband. She resolved not to burden them with her troubles as she herself had been burdened by her mother and was preoccupied with how the precarious condition of her marriage would affect them. The children's faces seemed to her to have "lost their light."

Other symptoms mirrored aspects of her own erotic attachment to and identification with her father, mobilized in part by the circumstance that both of her own daughters were of Oedipal age. Thus she was preoccupied with guilt about an actual extramarital affair, about fantasies of having affairs, and with suspicions that her husband was unfaithful. When the psychiatrist she saw briefly before hospitalization replaced his secretary, Mrs. White believed he did this in order to have an affair with her and came to believe that she was married to the doctor. Religious ideation and protestations about the "sanctity of marriage" expressed a guilt-dominated identification with her mother. Recurrent ideas that her husband was a latent homosexual expressed her own confused sexual identity in projective form. Thus, in the crisis preceding hospitalization, Kate White was confronted with various identification fragments (and defenses against them) which had previously remained in partial dissociation. These images of herself as a confused little girl in possession of secret and terrible information; as a long-suffering, neglected, and betrayed wife and mother; as a frustrated masculine careerist; as an Oedipally victorious daughter; and as a promiscuous philanderer were related to earlier identifications formed in relation to a frustrating and martyred mother; a prepossessing male mother-substitute; and a seductive, jealous, Oedipal father.

Two years subsequent to this hospitalization we learned that Mr. White had begun an affair with his secretary. He planned to keep up the appearance of a marriage for the sake of the children. Thus the earlier family drama was virtually replicated in the marital family.

ADULT DEVELOPMENTAL TASKS
AND THE CRISIS OF IDENTIFICATION

Kate White was thirty-six years old at the time of hospitalization and the mother of two girls, aged five and three. She had been married for a dozen years and had recently moved into a home of her own for the first time. Near midnight one evening she entered her church, took off her wedding ring, and placed it on the altar. This bizarre repudiation of her marriage symbolically located the area of her current troubles in the marital family.

From the very beginning Kate's marriage was marked by inner reluctance and uncertainty. Kate expected no consuming love in her life but decided to marry because it seemed like the appropriate thing to do. In college she had met a young man who had the same career interests that she and her father shared. She was feeling increasingly restive at home, in part because of the continuing eroticized attachment to her father, so that following college and a brief period of working she unenthusiastically accepted the young man's proposal of marriage.

The Whites began what was to be a prolonged phase of root-lessness as Nelson White wandered from job to job and town to town trying to find himself. Kate's role in the family was am-biguous. At times she was a competent career woman who helped support her husband's further education. At other times she deferred her career to his and depended on vicarious identifica-tion with his activities for a sense of accomplishment. Feminine domestic activities did not come easily and provided little sense of satisfaction and pride. In the face of her husband's preoccupa-tions with his own career to her exclusion, she felt abandoned, incompetent, and unloved.

Kate, as we have noted, had been a tomboy. She was active, outspoken, and rebellious, a replica of her father. Marriage now made demands for heterosexual intimacy and emotional involve-ment, for a more feminine participation in family life. She found herself unable to enjoy domestic roles or to perform them to her own satisfaction. She could not feel a sense of communality as a woman with her friends and neighbors. She could not fully trans-fer attachment from her father to a new man in a new family and felt increasingly alienated from her husband. Later, when she had children, she felt hopelessly tied down, frustrated in her career aspirations, and guilty about these feelings in relation to her daughters. She felt she would "go crazy" if confined to domestic routines. Elements of sexual confusion and dissatisfac-tion with her role as a woman also found representation, as we have mentioned, in the recurrent idea that her husband was a homosexual.

Concerns about marital infidelity also dominated her marital career. She often felt intense temptation and intense guilt over fantasies of affairs. She sometimes suspected her husband of in-fidelity and at one time felt "relieved" when her suspicions seemed to be confirmed—she had anticipated that this would happen to her and was reassured that it did not "shatter" her. It is worth considering in greater detail her one actual affair, as it played an important role in her preoccupations and in her pre-hospital crisis. The man was married and had children. It was he to whom she had been drawn before her marriage, but their incipient affair had been squashed by her father's intervention. This man visited her some years later, shortly after her father's death. Her marriage was in a state of silent isolation. Nelson White was away from home working in a distant city on one of many transient jobs. Kate was feeling lonely, unloved, and unappealing. Her husband's indifference to her and his outside interests had contributed to her sexual confusion. The man pressed his suit, Kate briefly felt more desirable and appreciated and engaged in a short affair.

Shortly afterward, Kate decided to have children. This decision was partially prompted by a desire to consolidate her marriage and support her insecure sexual identity. She hoped that the presence of children would involve her husband with the family and provide her with a sense of commitment to her role as a wife. Instead, motherhood increased her distress, dissatisfaction, and sense of alienation.

Some years later, just prior to her breakdown, this man visited her again and proposed an affair. During his visit she literally experienced the presence of her dead father in the house and discontinued the relationship. The visit came at a time of growing anxiety and sexual confusion as she faced "settling down" for the first time in a home of her own, as a wife and mother with a husband who seemed uninvolved with her and to whom she could not reach out for support of her precarious female identity. The other man's continued interest in her as a sexual partner provided both a reassurance and a danger; she sought hallucinatory gratification in the form of her father's return and protective concern for her.

Thus, marital life posed complex dilemmas for Kate White. She felt pulled in contradictory directions by a continued involvement with her father in the face of demands for transfer of this love to her husband, as well as by the presence of masculine identifications and homosexual trends which stood in opposition to the requirements of female heterosexual participation. The theme of infidelity and its associated identifications were also revived. Entry into marriage and motherhood imposed strategic and insurmountable developmental demands for the relinquishment of parental attachments and for the synthesis of conflicting identification elements in a workable adult identity.

MARITAL FAMILY PATTERNS AND THE CRISIS OF IDENTIFICATION

Through most of her marriage Kate White held to the view that her feelings of alienation and distress were the result of external uncertainties, in particular the rootless, almost nomadic life she and her husband were leading. She retained a hopeful fantasy of settling down to a secure place in a fixed community, of "sinking roots," and of thereby coming to feel at one with herself and her commitments. As we have seen, her severe personality disorganization began shortly after the Whites bought their first home and experienced, if only transiently, a sense that, after more than a decade of marriage, they were really settling down.

It is evident that the extended period of rootlessness had deferred for Kate White the necessity of synthesizing in herself incompatible identifications. It had also permitted her to deny the significance of her inner feelings, to avoid the terrible realization that she had always felt detached from people, empty, inadequate, and sexually confused. It had facilitated the projection onto her husband of her own sexual confusion and homosexual tendencies, of her inability to settle down and make firm commitments to adult roles and relationships, and of her promiscuous fantasies. The partial effectiveness of these defenses hinged on marital family patterns which could reinforce and support them. Perhaps the simplest way of designating the conjoint pattern of accommodation evolved by this husband and wife is as a state of suspension. By this we mean that the marital family accommodation was characterized by an explicit moratorium on commitments to personal and social roles, by ambivalent explorations of multiple careers and living situations, and by interpretations to each other that experienced troubles were the results of being "unsettled" and would be terminated in the future when roots would finally be established.

The White family was maintained for many years in this

state of suspension, supported by a myth of "becoming." They indicated by unspoken mutual agreement that lasting commitments were not made, that valued self-images were still to be sought in the future, and that existing unsatisfactory identities were only transient. Both husband and wife were exquisitely complementary in their sense of impermanence and in their continuing quest for adult identities. Nelson White's career line was marked by devious explorations and manifold uncertainties in the face of open horizons. He moved from good jobs in one field and locale to good jobs in other fields and locales and retained vague fantasies of returning to school someday to learn yet another profession. Kate White experimented with a career, marriage, and motherhood, constantly hoping for a sense of appropriate fit and meaningful commitment.

Nelson White gave little evidence of what he really was like or what his life plans were all about. He maintained a kind of distant ambiguity which provided little real contradiction for his wife's projections onto him. Indeed, his preoccupation with non-family matters, his occasional ambiguous hints of extramarital sexual interests, and his avoidance of a masculine role as effective head of the family furnished occasional support for her projections.

The style of marital life achieved by the Whites supported and maintained critical defensive structures for both partners. However, the consequences were double-edged. Although suspension of commitments avoided certain dangers, it simultaneously perpetuated the uncomfortable sense of personal role diffusion and social isolation. Nelson White's uncertainty in his career and his commitment to his marital role complemented Kate White's sense of estrangement, her sexual confusion, and her ambivalence about marriage and motherhood.

This form of marital accommodation could not survive without change the gradual aging of the marriage beyond that youthful period when the future seems to lie open and, most particularly, before the advent of children. With the birth of children Kate White reluctantly subordinated her career aspirations to meet the demands of motherhood. This change required a commitment which neither husband nor wife was able to make, and it emphasized for Kate the conflicts inherent in her identification with her father and lack of identification with her mother. Thus, when the couple finally attempted to settle down, in part because their older daughter was nearing school age, former patterns of family accommodation became increasingly untenable. Mr. White consented to purchase a home and for a time threw himself enthusiastically into his new work. After a time, however, he began to talk seriously about attractive career possibilities at a remote location and to lose interest in the daily requirements of his immediate job. Kate White, threatened by both the demand for commitment and the threat of impermanence, became increasingly disturbed. We may judge that the family could not relinquish that state of suspension which had served to accommodate each partner's conflicts and that the increasing necessity to do so served as one critical precipitant of what was at once a family crisis of commitment and a personal crisis of identification for Mrs. White.

CRISES OF IDENTIFICATION

In three other cases (Mark, James, Urey), marital life also reproduced a situation which corresponded to an earlier turning point in the wives' relations to their mothers. This repetition mobilized dissociated identifications with a characteristic content. The content included the mother as victim and as object of the child's anger. It also included the child as evilly responsible for the maternal loss and as a confused, helpless, and deprived victim. This constellation of parent-child identification was warded off until marital life revived it and undermined the previous defensive position.

Hilgard and her co-workers have focused on turning points constituted by parental loss through death or psychosis. In our small sample we encountered no instances of parental loss through psychosis. There were two instances of a mother's death in her child's early years, and both cases corresponded closely to the anniversary reaction hypothesis.

Irene James

Irene James was less than five when her mother became ill with a bad heart. The mother was bedridden for about a year and died at the age of forty. Irene thought that overwork in caring for the children had killed her. After the mother's death the family broke up. Four older siblings went out on their own; Irene and a slightly older brother lived in a series of foster homes, sometimes together, sometimes separately.

At twenty-two Irene married and gave birth to a daughter a year later. The birth was difficult, and Irene was ill during and right after the pregnancy. She feared dying. Irene described her marriage as neither happy nor conflictful—she and her husband were simply too young, they had very little in common, and they drifted apart. She sought divorce, and he agreed amicably; his mother consented to take care of the child. When Irene decided to divorce her husband and give up her child, the daughter was five, Irene's age when her mother died.

Irene remarried at thirty. Further trouble developed when she was thirty-five, her mother's age at her birth. Irene experienced severe abdominal pains and menstrual irregularities. She left the Catholic church, fearing that its teachings about divorce and sin would disturb her younger daughter and perhaps "split the family apart." Soon after this Irene became involved in a series of squabbles with neighbors which led to a decision to move. During her psychosis several years later, she interpreted the squabbles as part of a neighbor's complex plot to seduce her. It is not known whether these sexual fantasies were active at the earlier time.

Irene's psychotic episode began dramatically within a week of her fortieth birthday, which was her mother's age at the time of her illness and death. Irene fainted, attributed this to menstrual difficulties, and became convinced that she was entering the change of life. She experienced several events that she interpreted as snubs by neighbors and that she related to the earlier quarrels which she considered part of a seduction plot to break up her family. She was unable to work or sleep because of her preoccupations with the plot. After hospitalization she spoke of plots to make people sick and break up families, she noted the frequency of heart attacks at forty, and she had a reassuring dream in which her mother appeared and told her that doctors now have ways of curing illnesses that used to be fatal.

June Mark

June Mark is another illustration of the anniversary reaction hypothesis. June was the youngest of three girls. Her mother became seriously ill following the pregnancy with June and died when June was only four. June's main memories of mother are of climbing into the invalid's bed and being loved and caressed. June retained an idealized, almost saintly image of a generous, religious, and universally loved mother. Conversely, she retained an image of the maternal aunts who cared for her immediately following mother's death as cruel, ridiculing, and inclined to deprive her of things despite their wealth. She felt scorned as a shabby little orphan. Actually her mother's death was followed by extreme deprivation for June. After a brief stay with the wealthy aunts, the children moved about the country with their father as he traveled from one job to another. They were cared for by a series of housekeepers. They were very poor.

June's own difficulties became noticeable after the birth of *her* third daughter. She began to neglect the housework and to turn her attention from her husband to her children. She also felt a little weak, and her body did not seem quite right. Later, some months before hospitalization, June became concerned with the way in which some jealous, wealthy women in a community club were ridiculing and cruel toward her daughters. She became inordinately involved with the children, failing to come home from outings with them to fix dinner for her husband. She interrupted sexual relations to discuss the children's mistreatment by the cruel, wealthy ladies; she bought them extravagantly expensive gifts. June began to imagine that neighbors were gossiping about her, accusing her of sexual infidelity. She was hospitalized when her youngest daughter was four, her own age at the time of her mother's death.

Donna Urey

We also located a turning point constituted by parental infidelity, as in the case of Mrs. White, and by maternal abandonment, as in the following excerpt from the case of Mrs. Urey.

Donna Urey was the first of five children born to parents who did not marry until several years after her birth. After an extended period of irresponsibility, her father abandoned the family when she was six. Her mother had been extremely neglectful for many years and finally abandoned the children when she was twenty-six and Donna was eight, by calling on a social agency to take over because she felt unable to care for her children.

In the following years, Donna lived in an orphanage and then with a series of foster mothers. In each setting, she initially behaved in a helpful and appealing way, was well liked, experienced the foster mother as nurturant, and felt that she had found a good mothering person. Subsequently, she would experience the new mother as depriving, would become disobedient, and would run away. In each instance she ran toward a new home where she had already begun to form a new maternal attachment and where she believed she would find a good mother.

Early in her marriage, Donna began to feel lonely and neglected, her housekeeping deteriorated, and she began to hear voices accusing her of not properly caring for her children. Her experience of neglect and deprivation and the projected reproaches about her own mothering seem to replicate the anger she felt toward her own neglectful mother and her sense of deprivation as a child.

At twenty-six Mrs. Urey was hospitalized when she set fire to her home and said that she could no longer manage the care of her children. This was her mother's age at the time Donna was abandoned. At the time of hospitalization, Mrs. Urey had five children; her oldest, a daughter, was eight. At the time of her own abandonment, Donna, at eight, was the oldest of five children.

PERSONAL AND FAMILY
IDENTIFICATION CRISES

The dramatic coincidences of the anniversary reaction emphasize the special importance of a detailed repetition of an earlier situation in these crises and conversely de-emphasize the significance of contemporary marital family patterns. That this impression is not fully justified is suggested by the White case. Kate's struggle with an identification crisis in the marital family was shaped and molded by the conjoint participation of her husband in the establishment of a mutually meaningful pattern of accommodation. The accommodative pattern complemented the individual defense mechanisms of both partners. The accommodation, however, tended not only to support and maintain individual compromises to conflict, but also to perpetuate Mrs. White's precarious equilibrium, providing neither the opportunity for more successful mastery of earlier conflicts nor the possibility for simple regressive retreat. She remained in a situation of continuous conflict. The simultaneous coordination of increased pressure, both internal and external, for the integration of crucial identification and the disruption of family patterns of accommodation provided the occasion for both personal and family crisis.

In each of these cases, the marital relationship moved toward a pattern characterized by mutual withdrawal and inaccessibility of each partner to the other. This accommodation served the complementary defenses of the marital partners. As the wives' early conflicts were reawakened and intensified by progression into the marital and parenthood periods of life, the marital family solution of mutual withdrawal left them particularly vulnerable to the overwhelming revival of the past. Their actual marital relationships became limited and shadowy, fostering the confusion of present and past. Thus, in both the separation crises and the identification crises, interlocking or complementary defenses of the participants established marital family patterns which could not provide support against regression and which pressed competing claims for further progression.

PERSONAL STABILITY
AND THE MARITAL FAMILY

We have attempted to identify gross uniformities in the patterns of crisis experienced by the women we studied in the course of a critical transition into adult roles in marital families of their own. We have suggested that the inner obstacle to this transition in six cases was the strength of the maternal tie or the need for a type of symbiotic relationship modeled after this tie. In four other cases, the inner obstacle to this transition was the need to remain dissociated from a constellation of threatening identifications linked to the mother. We may say that the inner obstacles to participation in marital roles was in the one instance associated with movement out of childhood roles and in the other instance with movement—mediated by identifications with one's own mother and child—into dissociated childhood roles.

The marital family changes over time. Its members age, children are born into it and move through developmental stages echoing the parents' own histories, members become ill or depart or die, and events in the larger society impinge on it in changing ways. Two frequent stages in the early history of a marital family may be conceptually distinguished. The first is a two-party one-generation stage in which the most obvious task is the establishment of a new family unit with some integrity of external boundaries, some internal role division, and some achievement of a cross-sex reciprocity in love, work, and play. The normative solutions for these tasks vary widely from culture to culture and between social classes in our culture, but the tasks themselves are posed in some form by marriage. The second common early stage is the parental one in which a new generation is included in the marital family and must be cared for and socialized. Corresponding to these stages of marital history are successive roles for the adult family members, posing changing potentialities for personal gratification and threat for the occupants of each role. The first requisite is to establish an enduring cross-sex relationship as adult to another adult; the second, posed in the parental phase, is to participate as a father or mother in the socialization of children.

The successive tasks of early marital life each posed difficult problems for the wives we have described; both the marital task itself and the parental task evoked crises of varying magnitudes. The way in which these tasks were experienced, however, and thus the nature of the problems posed, differed for the separation and identification cases. In an important sense, wives experiencing a separation problem found that both stages of marital life posed a separation problem; wives experiencing an identification problem continued to experience an identification problem. Thus, although the setting and family roles changed, persistent inner pressures lent a similar meaning to the drama as a whole.

In the separation cases, the transition from the parental to the marital family was experienced as a struggle about leaving the mother and the role of daughter and establishing an identity as a separate adult. In each of these cases, the struggle was lost again and again. In various ways the marital family itself was transformed into something like a parental family, the role of daughter and child being sought and urged on the wife. These transformations always proved unstable, the conflicting interests of all the parties eventually moving the family back to equally untenable arrangements more closely approximating the normative model of marital life with its adult roles for husband and wife. The addition of children intensified the wife's and family's problem of separation. Thus in these cases a third-generation problem was posed by the conflict over who was the mother—the young mother or her mother—and who was the child—the young mother or her child. Only two roles were admitted where three were called for.

In the identification cases, on the other hand, the wives experienced difficulties in the two-party stage of marital life, primarily in the establishment of an appropriate female identity which would promote and sustain intimate heterosexual relations and feminine role performances. These difficulties seemed to be associated not with *leaving* mother, but with *being* mother or at least being some aspect of their internalized mother image. In the parental stage, this problem was exacerbated. Child-bearing and child-rearing pressed for the synthesis of identifications with the young mother's own mother. Further, identification with her own childhood self through her children proved threatening. Although we singled out the dominant threat posed by marital life in these cases as separation or identification, it is apparent that both problems assume importance in a given woman's life as the successive tasks of marriage and parenthood are encountered.

UNCLASSIFIED CASES

We did not classify seven cases as either separation or identification crises. These women also experienced severe difficulties as wives and mothers, but in some instances our knowledge about their marital lives was too vague or too ambiguous to warrant formulation.

Ann Rand

Ann Rand was thirty-six and her husband Louis thirty-seven at the time of her hospitalization. This was her second marriage and his first; they had been married for thirteen years. The family included two sons, aged eleven and six, and Ann's sixteen-year-old son by her first marriage.

Ann was the youngest of eleven children. Her father had had five children by a previous marriage; six more were born in his marriage to Ann's mother. Ann's father had done very well financially earlier in his life, but by the time Ann was born he had lost his business and his money and had moved with his family to another state, where he held a number of odd jobs. During and after Ann's infancy her mother had to work and was away from home much of the time. The older children fended for themselves and took care of the younger ones. Ann was babied and fussed over by her brothers and sisters, but they also teased her a lot, envied her, and excluded her from many of their activities. Ann's mother was an eccentric woman, very punitive and rejecting, and she had become a member of a fundamentalist religious sect just before Ann's birth. Thus Ann's mother would not celebrate the pagan rites of Christmas; Ann's father, however, made or brought gifts. The father was particularly fond of his baby Ann. But the parents could not get along together, argued bitterly, and separated when Ann was about six or seven. She received gifts from her father after that and saw him occasionally until he moved far away. He died when she was fifteen. Her mother became, if anything, increasingly odd and abusive after her divorce.

Ann married her first husband when she was eighteen and divorced him three years later, after having a son. Of this marriage she said only that her husband was very jealous, that he never wanted her to leave the house, and that, when she did so, he would question her in detail. It is not known whether she gave him reason to be jealous. She separated from him several times but did not seek divorce until she had met and planned marriage with Louis Rand. Her first husband wanted custody of the son, and Ann agreed to this.

The Rands married right after her divorce. Louis was a self-contained, even-tempered, conscientious, rather passive man. After the birth of their first son, Ann wanted to regain custody of her other son—then about five—and was able to do so. Another son was born when Ann was thirty, after seven years of marriage. We do not know whether there were any gross personal or marital difficulties during these years, nor do we know why major difficulties became apparent about two years before hospitalization. Ann had been increasingly restive, possibly about her youngest child's leaving babyhood, perhaps in response to an increasing sense of deprivation and isolation in her marriage. In any event, from the time she was about thirty-three, Ann started taking a diffuse series of courses at junior college, with some thought about a career out of the home. She began to complain to her physician of gastrointestinal pains, extreme nervousness, and insomnia. As the months passed, she felt herself to be on a merry-go-round; she was too busy but could not stop. She cried a great deal and felt very depressed and guilty. She had sinned, and her past would catch up with her. She had strong fears that she would lose control of herself. She felt unable to respond sexually. These symptoms waxed and waned but generally worsened over a two-year period during which her husband worked overtime, was minimally involved with her and the home, and ignored her difficulties. She was in a panic at the time of her hospitalization, very guilt-ridden, and convinced that she would die if she moved her bowels.

In other instances the present formulations did not seem to effectively describe the most salient issues. Two examples are considered here; further material about unclassified cases is available in the Appendix.

Peggy Sand

Peggy Sand was the oldest of eight children. Her family was very poor, moved a great deal, and sometimes lived in migrant workers' camps. She rarely spoke of her father; our impression is of a generally quiet, passive, ineffectual man. He died when Peggy was twenty. Her mother was clearly the dominant figure in the family, making the decisions, bossing the children, and complaining of her husband's inability to provide the decent things of life.

Peggy was eager to get away on her own from her early teens. She felt that her mother showed favoritism toward her brothers and sisters, and she rebelled against her mother's attempts to control her behavior. She ran around with young people her mother found objectionable, drank and stayed out to all hours, and was sexually promiscuous. She was only sixteen when she met Floyd, whom she married shortly thereafter despite her mother's disapproval.

The marriage was sadomasochistic. Peggy repeatedly provoked her husband into a fury by stubborn defiance, by secretly spending on herself money given her to pay bills, and by arousing his jealousy. They would have bitter fights, and he would beat her; their sexual relations were also characterized by resistance and attack. Often Peggy left Floyd after quarrels. In the first years of her marriage, she repeatedly went home to her mother; later she went to a sister's or a friend's home. One separation several months after the birth of their first child lasted nearly a year, during which time Peggy stayed with her mother and dying father. But most of the separations were brief and seemed to be part of a sadomasochistic interaction. During quarrels Peggy turned from her husband primarily to demonstrate his mistreatment of her and to punish him. In separation crisis cases, by contrast, we believe that the young women turned toward their mothers primarily out of guilt and out of feelings of emptiness and panic when alone or unsupported. In further contrast, Peggy was not an incorporative, overprotective mother to her own children.

The immediate precipitation of hospitalization was a furious argument between Peggy and Floyd. After the argument Peggy drove herself to the state mental hospital without informing her husband and asked for voluntary admission. She stated that she felt very upset and feared she might harm someone. Although Mrs. Sand was eventually diagnosed as schizophrenic, there is no evidence that she experienced the degree of immobilization or agitation found in other women we studied or that she ever had delusions or hallucinations. In this regard she also differed from the classified cases.

Rita Vick

Rita Vick was born out of wedlock when her mother was sixteen. She lived with her grandparents until she was three, when her mother married. From the time of her first stepbrother's birth two years later, Rita's behavior became difficult. She told lies, stole things, and would "run away to Granny" when there was trouble. She stayed away from school and lied about it to her parents. Reportedly they frequently beat her for her bad behavior and her lying. It should be mentioned that Rita gave us flagrantly contradictory accounts about her life at various times. However, because much of her disturbed adult life became the concern of social agencies, probation departments, the police, and the courts, we also had the records of independent observers.

Before she met Leo Vick, Rita, at twenty-five, had been married twice, had been promiscuous during and between marriages, and had had six children by four men. The first child, Tony, had been placed in a foster home by court order after the discovery of repeated instances of maternal neglect. Rita would leave him alone when she went out at night. Some of the other

children were in the legal custody of her second husband; Rita
had voluntarily placed the others in foster homes. Leo and Rita
met in a bar and began to live together within a week. Leo had
been married to a woman who had previously been married more
than once and who had frequently been unfaithful to him. To
Leo Rita seemed lonely and unhappy. He knew something of her
history and reputation but was going to rescue her: "The way I
saw it, she just put faith in the wrong kind of man." He married
her, and the couple soon moved into a new home they were buying. Mrs. Vick took formal steps to regain custody of Tony.
Tony's actual father, who had remarried and moved to a distant
state, came to California to actively oppose her and seek custody
himself. After the father won temporary custody, Rita would not
eat, cried, carried kitchen knives around, and muttered threats
to kill herself or to run away. She was hospitalized in the psychiatric ward of the county hospital in what appeared to be a state
of agitated depression. She calmed down quickly and was released
in less than a week.

This episode preceded admission to the state mental hospital
by three years. During these years Rita gave continuing evidence
of distress at the loss of Tony and made repeated efforts to win
custody. The sincerity of her interest in Tony was questioned by
the Probation Department, who mentioned abandonment of her
other children, especially Ronald, her last illegitimate son. Rita
then requested that Ronald be returned to her care. Within a
month of his return, Ronald had to be hospitalized because of a
serious accident which roused suspicions that he may have been
beaten. Later a court hearing gave custody of the still hospitalized and brain-damaged Ronald to his former foster parents and
concluded that the investigation of the accident had begun too
late to determine whether the child had been severely beaten or
merely grossly neglected. Shortly after this a court hearing gave
final custody of Tony to his father. Rita reacted to this decision
with violent rages and tantrums and talked of killing the people
involved in the decision. One night she called the police and
asked an officer to take her to the hospital because she was crazy
and had to get out of the house. The officer declined to take her,

but within two weeks she and Leo made arrangements for her voluntary admission to the state hospital.

In the next chapter we shall turn from the personal crisis of transition and its family setting to another level of analysis of the prehospital crisis. We shall again be concerned with family processes, but from the point of view of patterned family responses to withdrawal, illness, or distress in the wife. The emphasis will shift from family processes in relation to the wife's psychic conflicts to family processes in relation to the management of deviant behavior (including psychiatric illness), the seeking and use of professional help, and hospitalization. From this vantage point, we shall group the families in a somewhat different way than heretofore and shall find it possible to use many cases in which the personal significance of the crisis has resisted classification as a separation or identification crisis. As we shift our attention to the problem of family accommodations to deviance, we must keep in mind, however, that the accommodations in cases for which we could formulate the personal conflicts of the wives were *sources of,* as well as *responses to,* the wives' overt disturbance.

5

Becoming a Mental Patient

Family Processes

Becoming a psychiatric patient is not a simple and direct outcome of mental illness.[1] People who are by clinical standards grossly disturbed, severely impaired in their functioning, and even overtly psychotic may remain in the community for long periods without being recognized as psychiatrically ill and without benefit of any professional attention. Mental hospitalization, when and if it comes, is by no means the automatic result of a received professional opinion that it is advisable. In brief, the crisis leading to hospitalization cannot be understood in clinical terms alone; it is a socially structured event.[2] We shall attempt to contribute to an understanding of the social structure of the pre-

---

[1] This chapter is adapted from *The American Journal of Sociology*, LXVIII, No. 1 (1962), 86–96, and portions are reprinted with permission. Copyright 1962 The University of Chicago Press.

[2] Erving Goffman, "The Moral Career of the Mental Patient," *Psychiatry*, XXII (May 1959), 123–142, discusses a variety of "career contingencies" that may intervene between deviant behavior and hospitalization for mental illness.

hospital crisis by exploring the relationship between patterned family means for coping with the deviant behavior of a member who later became a mental patient and such formal means of social control as psychiatric help and hospitalization.

The broad nature of this relationship may be inferred from a number of published findings. Yarrow and her colleagues have documented the monumental capacity of family members, before hospitalization, to overlook, minimize, and explain away evidence of profound disturbance in an intimate.[3] The posthospital studies of the Simmons group have suggested that high "tolerance for deviance" in certain types of families is a critical determinant of the likelihood of poorly functioning and sometimes frankly psychotic ex-patients avoiding rehospitalization.[4] Myers and Roberts found that few mental patients or their families sought or used professional assistance before hospitalization until the problems they encountered were considered unmanageable.[5] Whitmer and Conover reported that the occasion for hospitalization was ordinarily not recognition of "mental illness" by the patient or his family but the family's inability to cope with disturbed behavior.[6]

These observations and our own permit two inferences. First, both before and after hospitalization some accommodative pat-

---

[3] Yarrow, Schwartz, Murphy, and Deasy, *op. cit.*

[4] James A. Davis, Howard E. Freeman, and Ozzie G. Simmons, "Rehospitalization and Performance Level Among Former Mental Patients," *Social Problems*, V, No. 1 (1957), 37–44; Howard E. Freeman and Ozzie G. Simmons, "Mental Patient in the Community: Family Settings and Performance Levels," *American Sociological Review*, XXIII, No. 2 (1958), 147–154; Simmons and Freeman, "Familial Expectations . . . ," *op. cit.; idem,* "The Social Integration of Former Mental Patients," *The International Journal of Social Psychiatry*, IV, No. 4 (1959), 264–271; *idem, The Mental Patient Comes Home, op. cit.*

[5] Jerome K. Myers and Bertram H. Roberts, *Family and Class Dynamics* (New York: John Wiley & Sons, Inc., 1959), pp. 213–220.

[6] Carroll A. Whitmer and Glenn C. Conover, "A Study of Critical Incidents in the Hospitalization of the Mentally Ill," *Journal of the National Association of Social Work*, IV (January 1959), 89–94; see also Edwin C. Wood, John M. Rakusin, and Emanuel Morse, "Interpersonal Aspects of Psychiatric Hospitalization," *Archives of General Psychiatry*, III (December 1960), 632–641.

tern ordinarily evolves between a psychiatrically disturbed person and his family, thereby permitting or forcing him to remain in the community despite severe difficulties. Second, it is the disruption of this pattern which eventually brings a disturbed person to psychiatric attention. An investigation of typical family accommodations to the deviant behavior of future patients and how these accommodations collapse should therefore contribute to our understanding of the ways in which individuals and the intimate social networks of which they are members are rendered more and less accessible to institutionalized devices of social control. Specifically, it should provide us with a glimpse of the family processes which determine a future mental patient's accessibility to the community, particularly psychiatric intervention. It should also contribute to our understanding of the meaning of intervention to the future patient and his family. Such family accommodations pose strategic problems to the people who constitute and man community remedial facilities.

In this chapter we shall discuss two phases in the relationship between the future patient and his family and the connections between these phases and the course of events leading to hospitalization. The first phase consists of the evolution of the family's accommodation to behavioral deviance on the part of the future patient. This phrasing emphasizes one side of a complicated reciprocity between family relations and the deviance of family members. We have focused on the other side of this reciprocity—family relations as they sustain and promote deviant behavior—in the preceding chapters. The second phase consists of the disruption of this accommodation. The patterns are exemplified by eleven and four cases respectively; two of the seventeen families do not appear to be adequately characterized by either pattern. We shall thus not exhaust the empirical variety to be found in even the limited number of cases before us here. As we shall emphasize in the concluding section of this chapter, however, the situations depicted suggest common patterns of relationship between future mental hospital patients and their immediate interpersonal communities, as well as the conditions under which these patterns deteriorate and collapse.

THE UNINVOLVED HUSBAND AND SEPARATE WORLDS

In the first situation, exemplified by eleven families—Baker, James, Mark, Oren, Price, Quinn, Rand, Sand, Thorne, Urey, and White—the marital partners and their children lived together as a relatively independent, self-contained nuclear family, but the marital relation was characterized by mutual withdrawal and separate worlds of involvement. At some point during the marriage, often quite early, one or both of the partners had experienced extreme dissatisfaction with the marriage. This was ordinarily accompanied by a period of violent, open discord; in other cases, the dissatisfaction was expressed only indirectly, through reduced communication with the marital partner. In either event, the partners withdrew from each other, and each gradually developed separate involvements.

The husband often became increasingly involved in his work or in other interests outside the marital relationship. The wife usually became absorbed in private concerns about herself and her children. In a variant instance—that of the Prices—the husband became absorbed in domestic matters and formed an intense emotional tie to his children while his wife withdrew into passivity and autistic preoccupations. The partners would rarely go out together, rarely participate together in personal or family problems, and seldom communicate to each other about their pressing interests, wishes, and concerns. The marriage would continue in this way for some time without divorce, without separation, and without movement toward greater closeness. The partners had achieved a type of marital accommodation based on mutual inaccessibility, emotional distance, and lack of explicit demands on each other. This accommodation represented an alternative to both divorce and a greater degree of marital integration. This type of family pattern gradually developed in all of the identification cases. It occurred in separation cases only in those two instances, where an ongoing triad, including a maternal figure, was not sustained. Thus the Price family moved from a marital organization resembling trigenerational merger, to a symbiotic husband-wife dyad which we termed conversion, to the pattern of mutual withdrawal which we are now considering.

It is a particularly important characteristic of mutual with-drawal that through it pathological developments in the wives were for a time self-sustaining. The wives' distress, withdrawal, or deviant behavior did not lead to immediate changes of family life but rather to an intensification of mutual withdrawal. In this setting, the wives became acutely disturbed or even psychotic without, for a time, very much affecting family life.

Donna Urey

In the evenings, Albert Urey worked on his car in the base-ment while his wife remained upstairs, alone with her sleeping children, engaged in hallucinatory conversations and arguments with imaginary people. In a recorded research interview, Albert Urey described his early experiences with Donna's "voices" in this way:

> MR. UREY: Well, at first she complained about them. Well, actually I do a lot of work in the base-ment and at night. I pick up a car now and then and work on it at home. At that particular time I was do-ing a lot of work on a car, and I spent most of my spare time in the basement. It got to the point where, just gradually—I mean, she wasn't one to complain—but it gradually got to the point where she believed that I had, well you might say, women down there with me. I mean she could hear women talking with me. And so, when that started, I knocked off right away. I mean, I just wouldn't go down there.
>
> INTERVIEWER: What did you tell her?
>
> MR. UREY: Well, I mean, I just told her it wasn't true, which it wasn't, and that, uh, that she knew bet-ter than that. But, uh, it was like I said, she would agree with me one minute and the next she would just turn right around and do the opposite.
>
> INTERVIEWER: Was she secretive about the voices?
>
> MR. UREY: Well, now, that's funny. After they actu-ally started, I mean at that time, she talked pretty

openly about it. And they would change. I mean they wouldn't be the same people all the time . . . and at the time, now I attributed it to the way the house was set. It was set back, and the street was fairly busy, and people were walking by. Their voices would echo in. I mean that's why I didn't think anything of it. I mean I just thought it was her imagination. . . . I mean, something like that, you know, I mean, right off the bat you don't really think anything's wrong.

This situation continued for at least two years before Donna Urey saw a psychiatrist on the recommendation of her family physician. Another two years elapsed before Donna was hospitalized. During this period, Albert became progressively less interested in his wife's behavior, accepting it as a matter of course, and concerned himself with his job.

Ann Rand

For two years prior to hospitalization, Ann Rand was troubled by various somatic complaints, persistent tension, difficulty in sleeping, a vague but disturbing conviction that she was a sinner, and intermittent states of acute panic. Louis Rand was minimally aware of her distress. He worked up to fourteen hours a day, including week ends, in his store, and a second job eventually took him out of the home three evenings a week. On those infrequent occasions when his wife's worries forced themselves on his attention, he curtly dismissed them as absurd and once again turned to his own affairs. An incident will serve to illustrate the nature of the marital interaction a few weeks preceding Ann Rand's hospitalization.

At lunch, Louis Rand announced to Ann that he would be working five rather than three nights a week. Ann said, "If you're gone all the time, I'll lose my mind." Louis answered, "Well, if you're going crazy, you're going to anyhow," and went back to work. After Louis returned to work, Ann decided to do some ironing.

I remember that I started to look for the ironing board, and I couldn't find it. I looked all over the house. I asked the kids to help me find it. They couldn't find it either. I went outside and looked around. I must have looked for about an hour. Then I came back in the house, and there the ironing board was standing right up in the kitchen. It frightened me. I felt I had wandered around in a daze. I called the doctor. He thought a lot of me, and I thought maybe he could recommend a psychiatrist. He wasn't in, and the person I talked to said I should go to the county hospital. In the meantime I called the church to talk to my minister, but he wasn't in either. So I talked to a friend in the church, and she came right over. She called another minister, and he came over, too. I was calmed down by then. The minister wanted to call my husband, but I told him not to. I know how Louis hates to be disturbed at work. They said they would take me to the county hospital, but I thought I'd wait until Louis came home. When he came home, he just laughed. He said, "Why that's silly. I lose things all the time. Other people do, too." I ended up not going anywhere.

In such families the response to withdrawal, illness, or distress in the wife was further withdrawal by the husband, resulting in increasing distance between and disengagement of the marital partners. It should be understood that these developments were neither abrupt nor entirely consistent, but that the trend of interaction in these families moved toward mutual alienation and inaccessibility. In this situation, early professional treatment for the wife was limited by the husband's detachment and by the wife's own withdrawal and difficulty in taking the initiative for any sustained action in the real world. The wife's treatment at a later time posed additional family issues.

The pattern of mutual withdrawal eventually became intolerable to one of the partners, pressure for a change was brought to bear, and the family suffered an acute crisis. In some cases, pressure for change was initiated by the husband. In other cases, the pressure was initiated by the wife in the form of increasing agitation, somatic and psychic complaints, and repeated verbal and behavioral communications that she was unable to go on. However, the prehospital crisis was initiated, and, whether its interpersonal significance signaled a desire for increased or reduced involvement by the initiating partner, the change indicated the incipient collapse of mutual withdrawal.

In four of the eleven cases considered here, the prehospital crisis was primarily precipitated by a shift in the husband's tolerance for deviance. In two of these cases, the wives had been chronically and pervasively withdrawn from role performances and at least periodically psychotic. Mr. Price, in the middle of job insecurities, a desire to move to another state to make a new start, and overinvolvement with his sons, became intolerant of his wife's chronic condition. Mr. Quinn, approaching forty, had been reassessing his life and decided that the time was now or never to rid himself of a wife whom he had long considered "a millstone around my neck." These husbands sought medical or psychiatric assistance specifically to exclude their wives from the family. The two wives were passively resistant to hospitalization. The explicit attitude of the husbands was that they wished the hospital to take their wives off their hands. Thus, Mr. Quinn remarked to the research interviewer less than two weeks after his wife was hospitalized:

> Well, I've had it, as far as this woman is concerned. I don't want her back interfering with my life and my children's lives anymore. I'm going to do everything that I can do to get the kids back to normalcy. Everything that has happened really had them confused. I don't want her back. I don't mean to say that I won't be responsible for her financially; I am. Morally, I will abide my conscience. But I have had it. She is capable of making a living, if she wasn't so goddamned lazy. She's lazy. Now, whether that is mental or not, I don't know. Frankly, I don't think her mind is put together the way the normal person's is.

As to how long she is going to be there, well, now the way it looks to me, this woman is a schizophrenia. That's the way it looks to me. I don't know if there are any drugs available to cure her personality traits or not. I have read that there are drugs for people who are in hilarity or depression. I would say this: Depending on the attitude of the patient, she would certainly be there a minimum of six months. Because this thing is not an overnight shot. It took years to accumulate; it will take years to pass off. I'm uncertain about whether she will get well. I don't think she will ever be completely well, frankly. Of course, who's to say on a mental thing who is well and who isn't.

In the other two cases, the disruption of the earlier accommodation was associated with the husband's serious extramarital liaison. In both cases the husband told his wife that he intended to press for divorce. As in the preceding two cases, prior to the husband's indication of a desire for total withdrawal, there appeared to be no marked change in the wife's pathology.

Cora Thorne

Cora Thorne reacted with acute distress to her husband's announcement that he intended to marry another woman. Some of her behavior at the time represented coercive or autistic attempts to preserve the marriage. She began to oblige her husband in areas of prior default—she rose to fix his breakfast for the first time in years; she indicated willingness to have sexual intercourse, which she had formerly avoided; she laid in provisions to entertain his friends, which she had formerly refused to do. Menstruation ceased, and Mrs. Thorne became convinced that she was pregnant. She speculated to herself, to relatives, and to a social worker whose help she sought that her husband really loved her and did not contemplate divorce but was testing her devotion in this way. She repeatedly expressed suicidal preoccupations to her husband and others.

Peter Thorne reacted to these changes with disbelief in their seriousness, by normalizing his wife's conduct, and by further withdrawing into his relationship with his girl friend. When Cora saw the social worker and then a psychiatrist, Peter made clear that this was her own business and explicitly sought to avoid any involvement in the treatment lest he be encouraged to abandon his plans. When others told him of his wife's distress, he responded that maybe this was so, but it must be happening when he wasn't around; she seemed "okay" to him.

One week-end morning, as Peter prepared to visit his girl friend, Cora made a serious suicidal attempt which failed only because of the speed of medical intervention. Mr. Thorne expressed astonishment because his wife was not "the suicidal type." After this incident, he ignored psychiatric advice to hospitalize her, doubting that the psychiatrist knew her well enough to assess the seriousness of her condition. Shortly thereafter, Cora attempted to kill one of her children, and this incident led to hospitalization.

Virtually identical family processes were apparent in the cases where the manifest illness of the wife was itself the source of pressure for change, the harbinger of the collapse of the prior marital accommodation. The wife's illness intruded itself into family life at first with limited impact, but then more insistently, like a claim which has not been paid or a message that must be repeated until it is acknowledged. The wife's "complaints" came to be experienced by the husband as, literally, complaints to him, as demands on him for interest, concern, and involvement. These husbands, however, all initially struggled to preserve the earlier pattern, that is, to maintain uninvolvement in the face of demands which implicitly pressed for their active concern. Thus, as the prehospital crisis unfolded, the wife's manifest illness became a demand for involvement, and the husband's difficulty in recognizing her as seriously disturbed became a resistance to that demand. The excerpt from the Rand case illustrated this process if we add to it the observation that, during the two years of Mrs. Rand's difficulties, the difficulties recurrently came to the husband's attention in the form of momentary crises which compelled at least the response of curt dismissal. In this situation, the husband initially assumed a passive or indifferent attitude toward his wife's obtaining professional help. But if she became involved with a psychiatrist, physician, minister, or social worker who took some interest in her situation, the husband became negatively concerned with the treatment. The treatment was not necessary, it was not helping, it cost too much money; along with these deprecations came a hint of alarm that the treatment would challenge the husband's uninvolvement. Thus Mr. Rand, whose working schedule was mentioned earlier, worried that the psychiatrist his wife had begun to see might support her complaint that he did not spend enough time at home. The involvement of the wife with a psychiatrically oriented helper was experienced by the husband, at least initially, as a claim on him—for money, for concern, and, most centrally, for reinvolvement. There is some basis for this feeling.[7] The treatment process, especially during hospitalization, does tend to induct the husband into the role of the responsible relative, thereby pressing for the re-establishment of expectations which had been eroded in the earlier family accommodation.

In most of these cases, these processes led to more extreme deviance on the part of the wife, eventually calling her behavior to the attention of the larger community and thereby resulting in hospitalization.[8] This effect seems to arise from the circumstance mentioned before—the wife's distress is experienced by the husband as an unwarranted demand for his reinvolvement in the marital relationship. Such a demand does not of itself significantly alter the husband's involvement; instead, it triggers further withdrawal.

[7] Harold Sampson, Sheldon L. Messinger, and Robert D. Towne, "The Mental Hospital and Marital Family Ties," Social Problems, IX (1961), 141–155.

[8] Edwin C. Wood, John M. Rakusin, and Emanuel Morse, "Interpersonal Aspects of Psychiatric Hospitalization. I," Archives of General Psychiatry, III (1960), have arrived at a related conclusion on the basis of an analysis of the circumstances of admission of forty-eight Veterans Administration patients. "There is also evidence to suggest that hospitalization can for some patients be a way of demanding that those close to them change their behavior, just as it can be an expression by relatives that they are dissatisfied with the patients' behavior" (p. 640).

A few weeks after the ironing board incident, Ann Rand woke her husband and told him she could not sleep. He reportedly told her that he was tired and urged her to try to sleep. Just before dawn she arose, wrote her husband a brief note "so as not to interrupt his sleep," and drove to church. She entered the minister's office, said, "God help me!" and collapsed into tears. Once again, when the minister wanted to call her husband, she urged not disturbing him. This time the minister disregarded her. Within an hour a now worried and concerned husband was at the e, and arrangements were under way to hospitalize .

In each of these cases, the prehospital crisis marked and was part of the disruption of a pattern of accommodation which had been established between the marital partners. The disruption was in effect initiated by one of the partners and resisted by the other. The former accommodation and the way in which it came to be disrupted were important determinants of the processes of recognizing the wife as mentally ill, of seeking and using professional help, and of moving the wife from the status of a distressed and behaviorally deviant person in the community to that of a mental patient. These processes, in fact, can be understood only in the context of these family patterns. The problem of early intervention in cases of serious mental illness and of effective intervention in the later crises which ordinarily do come to psychiatric attention cannot be formulated meaningfully without consideration of the interpersonal processes which determine when, why, and how sick people become psychiatric patients.

THE OVERINVOLVED MOTHER

In a contrasting situation found in four cases—Arlen, Karr, Low, and Yale—the marital partners and their children did not establish a relatively self-contained nuclear family. Rather, family life was chronically or periodically organized around the presence of a maternal figure who took over the wife's domestic and child-rearing functions. This person was the wife's mother in three cases, her mother-in-law in the fourth (Arlen). (The distinction is not critical in the present context, and we shall refer to "the wife's mother.") These are the separation cases in which family organization moved toward trigenerational merger or repeatedly oscillated between merger, relative independence, and the wife's returning alone to her mother.

This organization of family life was a conjoint solution to the interlocking conflicts of the wife, husband, and mother. These mothers were possessive and intrusive, wanted to perpetuate their daughters' dependency, and were characteristically disposed to assure the "helpful" role in a symbiotic integration with her. The daughters ambivalently pressed for the establishment or maintenance of a dependent relationship to their mothers and struggled to break the inner and outer claims of the maternal attachment. The husbands responded to anxieties of their own about the demands of heterosexual intimacy and marital responsibility, as well as their own ambivalent strivings toward maternal figures, by alternately supporting and protesting their wives' dependence on the maternal figure. The resulting family organization, in which the mother was intermittently or continually called on for major assistance, represented an alternative to both a relatively self-contained, independent nuclear family and to permanent marital disruption with the wife returning to live with the parental family.

In direct contrast to the family accommodation described in the preceding section, the wives in triadic families did not quietly drift into increasing isolation and autism. Here, sickness or withdrawal by the wife were occasions for intense maternal concern and involvement. This development was ordinarily abetted by the husband. The resulting situation, however, would come to be experienced as threatening by the wife. She would come to view her mother as interfering with her marriage and her fulfillment of her own maternal responsibilities, as restricting her freedom, and as preventing her from growing up. At this point a small but often violent rebellion would ensue, and the husband would now participate with his wife to exclude or limit the mother's participation in family life. Such cycles of reliance on the mother followed by repudiation of her recurred over the years with only minor variations.

This accommodation complicated seeking and using professional help, but in a distinctively different way than in the family setting depicted earlier. Here, in response to withdrawal, illness, or distress in the wife, the mother replaced the wife in her domestic and child-care functions and established with the wife a characteristic integration involving a helpless one who needs care and a helpful one who administers it; the husband withdrew to the periphery of the family, leaving the wife and mother bound in symbiotic interdependency. To cite one example, when Mrs. Karr returned home after the birth of her second child, she developed intense breast pains. Her mother, who lived next door, came to stay with her, took over the care of Mrs. Karr and the children, and ran the household. Mr. Karr moved out of the house temporarily. This response did not simply make outside help superfluous for a while; more to the point, outside help constituted a threat to the existing interdependency of mother and daughter, carrying the implication that it was inadequate or unnecessary or even harmful. In the previously described family accommodation, treatment came to be experienced as a threat to the husband's uninvolvement; here, treatment was a threat to the mother's involvement.

It was the failure of this family accommodation which led to the wife's contact with the physician or psychiatrist. This failure occurred when, simultaneously, the wife rebelled against the maternal attachment, but was unable to establish with her husband the previously effective alternative of temporary repudiation of that attachment.

We observed that Mrs. Yale's mother came to consider her seriously emotionally disturbed and in need of professional help when the daughter began to express open resentment about the mother's "helpfulness." In all of these cases, the behavior which led family members to doubt the young woman's sanity consisted of hostility, resentment, and accusatory outbursts directed toward her mother. In these violent outbursts toward the maternal figure, the daughter was indeed "not herself." It was at just this point that the daughter's behavior constituted a disruption of the former family pattern of accommodation and led to involvement with outside helpers. The mother might now view outside helpers as potential allies in re-establishing the earlier interdependency; the psychiatrist, however, was unlikely to fulfill the mother's expectations in this regard, and then he became an heir to the husband in the triadic situation, a potential rival to the mother-daughter symbiosis. This sequence has been documented in detail in the Yale case.

We may summarize, then, certain connections between this type of family accommodation and the use of professional help prior to hospitalization. The initial response of the family to the wife's distress was to attempt to reinstate a familiar pattern: a drawing together of mother and daughter in symbiotic interdependency and a withdrawal of the husband to the periphery of the family. This accommodation was disrupted by the eruption of the daughter's formerly ego-alien resentment toward her mother, and at this point the mother was likely to view physicians or psychiatrists as potential allies in restoring the former equilibrium. The psychiatrist, however, was unlikely to play this part and became, for the mother, a rival to the interdependency. For the daughter, also, this meaning of treatment invested it with the dangerous promise of a possible separation from the maternal figure. In this drama the husband was likely to play a relatively passive if not a discouraging role, affording the wife little if any support in what she experienced as a threatening and disloyal involvement outside the family.

The way in which the hospitalization of the wife came about in the collapse of this family accommodation also contrasted to the processes depicted in the preceding section. As the prehospital crisis developed, the wife sought to withdraw from continuing intolerable conflict in the triadic situation. At first she felt impelled to choose between regressive dependency on a maternal figure and the claims of her marital family but unable to either relinquish the former or achieve inner and outer support for the latter. Both alternatives were transiently affirmed and repudiated in the period preceding hospitalization, but in time she came to feel alienated from *both* her mother and her husband and driven toward increasing psychic withdrawal. This process did not resolve her conflicts or remove her from the triadic field, and in time she herself pushed for physical removal.

Thus, in two of the four triadic cases, the wife herself, with a feeling of desperation, explicitly requested hospitalization (Yale and Arlen). In a third case, the disturbed wife was brought to a psychiatrist in the company of both mother and husband, refused to return home with them after the appointment, and was thereupon hospitalized (Karr). In the fourth case (Low) the wife was initially cooperative to a hospitalization plan, but equivocation by the husband and psychiatrist delayed action, and the wife gave herself and her daughter an overdose of drugs, thereby precipitating the hospitalization. Only this last case resembles the most common pattern described in the preceding section, in which the wife is driven to extreme deviance which comes to the attention of the larger community and compels hospitalization. The second pattern, in which a husband takes primary initiative for hospitalizing a reluctant wife because she has become a "millstone around my neck," was entirely absent.

ACCOMMODATIONS TO DEVIANCE

The career of the mental patient and his family ordinarily comes to the attention of treatment personnel during the course of an unmanageable emergency and again fades from view when that emergency is in some way resolved. Prior to this public phase of the crisis and often again after it, the disturbance of the patient is contained in the community. It is the collapse of accommodative patterns between the future patient and his personal community which renders the situation unmanageable and ushers in the public phase of the prehospital (or rehospitalization) crisis.

Our analysis has been addressed to ways in which two particular organizations of family life have contained pathological processes, to the ways in which these organizations were disrupted, and to the links between family processes and recognition of illness, seeking and using professional help, and the circumstances of mental hospitalization. The analysis carries us beyond observations that families often tolerate deviant behavior and resist recognition, that the future patient is seriously disturbed and may be reluctant to use help, toward a view of typical accommodations around deviance and typical forms of the pre-hospitalization crisis.

It is, of course, by no means evident how typical the patterns we have described are. Although the analysis is confined to certain marital family organizations and does not entirely exhaust even our own empirical materials, we may raise the possibility that the presentation does touch on two frequently encountered situations in work with the mentally ill and their families. In the first situation described, the future patient and his immediate personal community move from each other, effect patterns of uninvolvement, and reciprocate withdrawal by withdrawal. The future patient moves and is moved toward exclusion from personal ties and from any meaningful links to a position in communal reality. This situation, as we have seen, is compatible with very high tolerance for deviant behavior, which may permit an actively psychotic patient to remain *in* the community while not psychosocially *of* it.

The accommodation may be disrupted by a shift in the tolerance of the personal community, however determined, or from the future patient by increasing agitation which in part signals an attempt to break out of inner and outer isolation. Here, hospitalization is a possible route toward further disengagement of the patient from his personal community or, conversely, toward re-establishment of reciprocal expectations compatible with re-engagement. Whatever the outcome, a strategic therapeutic problem is posed by the chronic pattern of mutual disinvolvement and withdrawal.

In the second situation, the future patient and a member of his immediate interpersonal community become locked in mutual involvement, effect patterns of intense interdependency, and reciprocate withdrawal by concern. The future patient moves and is moved toward a bond in which interlocking needs tie the participants together rather than isolate them. This situation is also compatible with high tolerance for deviant behavior, but here because the deviance has become a necessary component of the family integration. It is this type of family process, rather than the first type, which has attracted most psychiatric interest, although there is no reason from our data to suppose that it is the more common.

In the cases observed, the disruption of this accommodation took the form of an ego-alien movement by the future patient against the claims of the prepossessing attachment. Here, hospitalization is at once an escape from intolerable conflict in the personal community and a potential pathway toward re-establishing the earlier pattern of accommodation. The strategic therapeutic problem posed is the contrasting one of modification of a chronic pattern of intense involvement.

The observations reported do not yield precise knowledge as to how psychiatric intervention might routinely be brought about earlier in the development of a serious mental illness, whether or when this is advisable, and how intervention might be more effective later on. The observations indicate, rather, that we must confront these questions in their actual complexity and investigate more closely and persistently than heretofore the characteristic ways in which families cope with severe psychiatric disturbances, the ways in which the intrafamily mechanisms are disrupted, and the significance of the family dynamics which form the crucial background of the eventual encounter between patient and clinician.

6

Crisis Resolutions

Hospital and After

We have been considering progressive personal and familial disorganization which led to mental hospitalization.[1] At the moment of admission, most of the wives were confused, withdrawn, and very frightened. Their family ties were disrupted and seemed in permanent jeopardy. The immediate past and present were painful and unreal; no tolerable future could be believed. For the husbands, also, hospitalization marked a turning point into an unknown future. Would the wife ever recover? Would she then return to the family? When? In what condition? What did the children know, and what should they know? Could—and should—efforts be made to forget and undo disruptive and alienative acts and bitter words? Whatever his private hopes or fears, the husband inevitably experienced a sense of uncertainty, of waiting on unforeseeable developments. He also found it

[1] This chapter is based in part on two previous articles: "The Mental Hospital and Marital Family Ties," *Social Problems*, IX, No. 2 (1961), 141–155, and parts are reprinted with permission of the publisher; and "The Mental Hospital and Family Adaptations," *The Psychiatric Quarterly*, XXXVI (1962), 704–719, reprinted in part with permission of the publisher.

difficult to envision and believe in a predictable and coherent future. In time, however, these wives and husbands did re-establish, together or separately, some tenable scheme of living. New adaptations were tentatively worked out which required psychological reorganization and the restructuring of relationships. These new adaptations are what we mean by crisis resolutions.

OVERVIEW

The median length of stay in the state hospital from first admission to first release was about four months. The shortest hospitalization was six weeks. Only one woman was hospitalized for more than a year, and she was placed on leave of absence sixty-four weeks after admission. The women spent a few days to a couple of weeks in the admission ward and were then assigned to the acute treatment ward, from which most were released to the community. Ten women were briefly removed from these wards at some time during their stay and placed in the disturbed ward in the admission building.

During hospitalization all of the women spent some time in small discussion groups designated as group psychotherapy and participated in other organized group activities. Most received very limited and intermittent drug treatment. Ten received electroshock therapy but in only three cases was a full course of twenty treatments administered. None received individual psychotherapy.

Some clinical improvement could be observed in all cases, and the wives were released in states of partial to complete remission of overt symptoms. In some cases, the clinical picture at release was of tenuous suppression of disturbing affects and ideas, concealment or isolation of residual psychotic symptoms, and continued reliance on projective defenses. At the other extreme, relatively effective repressions were reinstituted, the patient was amnesic for the episode and the "sick" period of hospitalization and troubled in daily living by memory gaps and inefficiencies.

Some restoration of deteriorated family relationships usually occurred during hospitalization. Role expectations between the marital partners were rebuilt in a graduated, trial framework. At first, husband and wife were permitted to see each other only briefly and in the hospital ward, a setting which drastically limited the possibilities and demands of marital interaction. The children were not allowed to visit the hospital ward. After transfer to the acute treatment ward, the patient could apply for a pass home and was likely to receive one within a few weeks. Usually the first pass did not permit her to remain away from the hospital overnight. On these short passes, the husband sometimes did not take his wife home, but rather to a nearby town to eat and wander about until it was time to return. The pass was sometimes spent on the hospital grounds. In several instances, the children were not seen on these first passes.

If early encounters did not disturb either the patient or her husband too severely, subsequent visits were longer, and the wife tended to assume some of her domestic duties. On a three-day–week-end pass, the husband generally went to work on Monday, and the wife cared for the children alone during the day, prepared her husband's dinner that evening, and then returned to the hospital. Changes in the marital relationship will be considered later in some detail. Here, it is sufficient to note that in fourteen of seventeen cases the wife returned to the marital family at release and resumed for at least a time her roles as wife and mother.

The early posthospital period was characterized by continued personal and family instability. We may sketch certain posthospital trends by discussing "survival" in the community, in the marital family, and in a functioning adult role in or out of the marital family.

Survival in the Community

Survival in the community is an important social criterion and is, of course, very meaningful to the patient as well as to his society. It is not, however, determined solely—and perhaps not even primarily—by psychiatric status and is not precisely correlated with the quality and level of posthospital adjustment. In a follow-up survey of a sample of veterans, Wood, Rakusin, Morse, and Singer found that rehospitalized and not rehospitalized patients differed in family setting, but not in psychiatric symptoms or impairment.[2] The "Minnesota Follow-up Study" found that factors related to rehospitalization are relatively independent of factors associated with good adjustment.[3] In the series of studies cited earlier, Simmons and his colleagues demonstrated that the ability to remain in the community at a low level of functioning and in spite of psychotic symptoms critically depends on the tolerance of the family setting. In our work, we have seen patients who remained in the community for extended periods before as well as after hospitalization, while overtly psychotic and virtually unable to carry on any adult role functions. We have attempted to link this phenomenon to specific family patterns of accommodation. With these important qualifications in mind, we may turn to rehospitalization data. Six months after first release, fifteen of the seventeen patients had remained in the community continuously; two (Price and Vick) had been rehospitalized. Within twelve months, a third patient (Noon) had been rehospitalized. Sixteen months after release, the last point at which we have reliable data on this item across all cases, a fourth patient (White) had been rehospitalized. Available data indicates that at least two additional cases (Urey and James) were rehospitalized subsequently, at eighteen and twenty-two months after release respectively. Thus at least six patients were hospitalized again within two years of first release. In four of these cases, there was more than one rehospitalization in the follow-up period.

The rehospitalizations varied in length. They testify, however, to continued personal and family instability after the first release. Moreover, it would be accurate to say that in the six cases there was an erosion, through the period of posthospital observation, of the patients' ties to the marital family and, more broadly, to functioning adult roles in the community. Thus, although not

[2] Edwin C. Wood, John M. Rakusin, Emanuel Morse, and Ruth Singer, "Interpersonal Aspects of Psychiatric Hospitalization. III The Follow-Up Survey," *Archives of General Psychiatry*, VI (1962), 46–55.

[3] "Minnesota Follow-Up Study Summary" (Unpublished report, 1961).

being rehospitalized does not indicate successful readjustment, the rehospitalizations observed seemed to us to be part of a progressive disengagement from the community.

Survival in the Marital Family

Let us turn to survival in the marital family. Fourteen women returned to their marital families at release; three were separated. In two cases (Baker and Quinn) a divorce was obtained; in the third (Thorne) a marital reconciliation was effected shortly after release, and the marriage remained intact through the period of our follow-up.

We shall consider the marital family status of the seventeen women at the time of our last reliable information in each case. This method of presentation does not define a risk group with equal exposure to likelihood of change in status, as the time of follow-up varies from twelve months to well over two years. If this limitation is kept in mind, the summary has the advantage of using all the information we do have. It is misleading only if interpreted as a statement of the marital vicissitudes of the group over a uniform time. It should be added that, aside from the changes in status associated with rehospitalization, in only one case of extended follow-up was there a change in family status after the first twelve months after release.

At the time of last follow-up, seven women were not living in the marital family. Four of the seven (Price, Noon, James, and Urey) were in the hospital but still formally married; the objective situation and the psychological status of the marital relationship alike lead us to consider these as instances of unofficial separation. We mean to imply by this that the idea of marital reconciliation had faded in these families and that mental hospital patienthood was becoming a customary way of life for the wife. Two of the seven (Vick and Quinn), one of whom had been rehospitalized earlier and then released, were living alone in the community; their children were in the care of the husband. The last of the seven (Baker) was living with one child in the community; her other child lived with her former husband.

Three women were living in the marital family at the time

of last contact, but after prior separations. Mrs. Thorne was separated from her husband at the time of release, and a reconciliation took place later. Mrs. Yale and her husband separated several months after her release and were reconciled about a year later. Mrs. White had been rehospitalized twice during a very stormy posthospital period. At the time of last follow-up, two years after first release, she had just returned to her husband on leave of absence after a six-month hospitalization. Her husband had informed her that he had an extramarital liaison which he intended to continue and that he would maintain the marriage only for the sake of the children. Mrs. White's personal adjustment seemed tenuous, and the future of the marriage was clearly in question.

Seven women (Arlen, Karr, Low, Mark, Oren, Rand, and Sand) were living in the same marital family at time of last contact and had been continuously since release.

Survival in a Functioning Adult Role

Seven women were not living in the marital family at time of last contact. Of these, only Mrs. Baker was functioning in the community in any adult roles. She was working, assuming some responsibility for care of one of her two children, and had become engaged to remarry.

Of the ten women living in the marital family at the time of last contact, eight were functioning as wives and mothers, apparently as well or better than during much of their prehospital lives. As far as we could determine, they were relatively free of overt psychotic symptoms. The other two women—Mrs. White and Mrs. Mark—had been intermittently psychotic during most of the postrelease period and were virtually disengaged from participation in marital family roles. Mrs. Mark was not rehospitalized during a two-year–follow-up period.

CRISIS RESOLUTIONS

This brief sketch of certain hospital-posthospital vicissitudes of the study group affords a gross overview of crisis resolutions. For many of the women—about half of our small study group—

the initial hospitalization marked a stage in a continuing process of disengagement from participation in communal reality, a process moving over time toward a regressive reorganization of living. Whether the regressive reorganization was forming around chronic hospital patienthood or not, whether officially remaining married or not, this group of women moved and was moved toward exclusion from adult roles and strivings. For another group of cases, about equally large, the direction of crisis resolution over time was not regressive. After a period of uncertainty and anxious exploration of alternatives, they re-established something like the *status quo ante* or fashioned more-or-less altered relationships in which they appeared to have achieved some stability and satisfaction.

We shall look more closely at typical crisis resolutions and the forces which shaped them by examining what happens during and after hospitalization to patterned marital family accommodations. This approach will permit a view of the direction of personal and family reorganization in some detail while transcending the biographical specificities of the individual case. It will also permit the best use of our data with their special virtues of relatively good cross-case coverage of family processes and extended career sequences and their special limitations in uniform cross-case data in depth about subtle clinical fluctuations and psychodynamic shifts.

The accommodative patterns described earlier were based on relatively overt, gross aspects of relatedness between the patient and her intimates and proved for that reason applicable to most of the cases studied. This level of analysis permitted us to go beyond the fewer number of cases treated more intensively and more psychologically as crises of separation and identification. These accommodative patterns also seemed to us to represent two classic situations encountered in work with seriously ill psychiatric patients, situations posing rather different management and therapeutic problems. In the first situation, the patient has been caught in a pathological tie to an overinvolved intimate; in the second, the patient has moved and been moved through mutual withdrawals toward exclusion from personal ties. This approach to the description of crisis resolutions directs attention to processes which are rarely the subject of systematic inquiry and conceptualization and are not part of the traditional schemes of explicit diagnosis, treatment, and evaluation of results. Nonetheless, it provides us with an instructive and potentially useful way of examining reorganizational processes associated with hospitalization and return to the community.

The occasion for hospitalization is social as well as clinical; it includes a breakdown of a prior accommodation between the patient and his personal community as well as a breakdown or further disruption of his intrapersonal mechanisms of defense. Thus the reorganizational process and the crisis resolution effected must include either a repair of the social breakdown or the establishment of an alternative scheme of living in a new social setting.

It is not very presumptuous, furthermore, to argue for the intimate connection between changes in the relationships in the patient's family and the direction of his psychic reorganization. The reorganization of family patterns is a reorganization of the fabric of the patient's life. It is more difficult, of course, to convert this generality into an explicit analysis of these connections, and we shall not be entirely dismayed if our own work can provide only crude and uneven beginnings in this task.

Finally, the changes in family relationships which concern us have important bearings on the posthospital world. The adjustment tasks and possibilities the patient encounters after release, as well as his likelihood of remaining in the community, are concretely determined by the setting to which he returns. Does crisis resolution move in the direction of a restoration of former patterns, thus perhaps confronting the ex-patient with a similar situation to that in which his illness developed? Or does crisis resolution favor a reorganization of family life which poses new possibilities, new dangers, or new limitations for the released patient?

These considerations, as well as the special characteristics of our data, lead us to describe crisis resolutions in terms of changes in the relatively enduring patterns of integration between the patient and her intimates rather than in terms of her clinical condition by itself.

The Marital Family Triad

We have characterized the prehospital organization of family life in four cases as marital family triads. The marital partners and their children did not function as a relatively self-contained nuclear family. Rather, family life was organized around the availability of a maternal figure who would intermittently take over the wife's domestic and child-rearing functions. In three cases, this person was the wife's mother; in the fourth (Arlen), her mother-in-law.

The patterned response of family members to any distress on the part of the wife was for the mother to assume the wife's family tasks and to establish with her a characteristic integration involving a helpless one who needed care and a helpful one who administered it. The husband would actively or passively encourage this arrangement, withdraw to the periphery of family life, and leave mother and wife mutually bound in symbiotic interdependency. The long-term prehospital trend was for the marital family to organize increasingly around an enduring mother-daughter interdependency. This trend was disrupted during the immediate prehospital crisis, and hospitalization followed on, and was related to, the wife's withdrawal from both mother and husband. The disruption took the form of bitter reproaches and accusations by the daughter against the maternal figure. The mother experienced these outbursts as bizarre, and they were actually eruptions of ego-alien affects and impulses. They signified the daughter's desperate struggle against an overwhelming and dangerous attachment rather than the achievement of even a limited degree of emotional distance from the claims of that attachment. This pathological development was abetted by the wife's inability to find in her marital relationship any viable alternative to the threatening maternal tie, for the husband would respond to her dependency or her movements toward intimacy by withdrawal and encouragement of her involvement with her mother. We wish to explore here the direction and stability of changes in this pattern during and after hospitalization and to connect such changes to institutional processes where a link appears to exist.

There is a striking uniformity in the direction of reorganization observed in the four triad cases. In each, the hospitalization reinforced the disruption of the triadic pattern; the husband and wife drew more closely together and attempted to achieve a greater measure of independence from the maternal figure. This uniform direction of change is illustrated by a brief excerpt from the case of Mrs. Yale, whose prehospital patterns are already familiar.

> Shortly before release, Mrs. Yale haltingly told the research interviewer that her attachment to her mother had interfered with her marriage and that she planned to maintain both geographical and emotional distance from her mother. She said that she and her husband were able to talk more calmly now and to take greater perspective on their marital problems. They were resolved to participate in more shared activities, to try to make their marriage succeed, and to live in an independent household far from her mother. The mother, at this time, had established residence with another relative in a distant city. Mr. Yale confirmed his wife's view of marital changes and emphasized his wish to maintain a separate marital household. He claimed that his wife seemed more emotionally independent of her mother, and he noted that for the first time in years he felt spontaneously affectionate toward his wife.

The observed similarity of outcome in even so few cases as we are considering is provocative. How may we begin to understand it? We should like to consider the possibility that institutional processes associated with mental hospitalization in some way favored the observed direction of change. We shall develop this line of thought, but certain prefatory comments are in order.

The links we propose between institutional processes and

changes in the triadic pattern are plausible, but they are derived after the fact and from very few cases. They cannot be verified without systematic, controlled investigation. They are offered as hypotheses which warrant further study, hypotheses which may contribute to the conceptualization of the effects of mental hospitalization on family processes. These effects are not the result of case-specific procedures applied with conscious deliberation by treatment personnel, but are consequences of implicit features of hospitalization. They stand outside our usual field of observation and deliberate intervention but, if our view is correct, not at all outside the critical field of forces which shape the direction of crisis resolution.

An immediate concomitant of hospitalization was the factual and official transfer of the care of the wife to people outside the family. This very obvious change constituted a replacement of the former triadic pattern of accommodation with a functional alternative. The mother was displaced by the hospital, and the mother-daughter interdependency was weakened in several ways. The provision of an alternative source of care and treatment for the wife created a situation in which she could struggle against the inner claims of the maternal attachment in circumstances of reduced reality dependence and reduced interpersonal reinforcement. Hospitalization thus lessened the desperation of this struggle. In each case, ego-alien rebellion was gradually replaced by a tentative, more realistic striving for greater emotional distance as a condition of greater independence. The following comment by Mrs. Low shortly after release is typical:

> I think that my mother—my attachment to my mother—probably had a lot to do with my not having a very successful marriage, and I somehow think that after the breakdown and my decision that I wasn't going to go home and I was going to stay with him instead sort of was the breaking point of whatever—I think my mother then understood too. . . .

Hospitalization also provided the mother with opportunities to free herself from the interdependency. It would be misleading to characterize these manifestly intrusive, overpossessive mothers as simply seeking to cling to their daughters. On close observation, both partners seemed to be simultaneously willing and unwilling prisoners of a stereotyped relation. The daughter's helplessness, dependency, and illness had been claims on the mother, claims which she accepted in a fusion of genuine concern, guilt, hostility, and secret gratification. The husband's abdication of responsibilities was also a source of genuine anxiety to the mother, as well as of secret gratification that after all she alone loved and was indispensable to her troubled child. The mental hospital was also experienced ambivalently as a dangerous rival which might turn the daughter against the mother, as a depreciated rival unable to match a mother's love, and as a helpful alternative to a mutually limiting bondage.

The daughter's hospitalization afforded the mother new opportunities for disengagement, and to some extent each mother did withdraw transiently from the symbiotic integration. Mrs. Yale's and Mrs. Low's mothers remained out of town through most of the hospitalization and into the early posthospital period, although indicating their strong hope that after release their daughters might take up life near them rather than alone with their husbands. Mrs. Karr's mother visited her daughter infrequently during hospitalization and was somewhat less intrusive than usual following release. Mrs. Arlen's mother-in-law became more circumspect in intervening in the marital family's affairs. The partial withdrawal of these mothers was not only a result of their readiness to accept an opportunity for disengagement, but was also a reaction to the daughters' hostility and reduced willingness to confide or seek assistance.

In addition, the mothers had reduced opportunities to intervene actively during the hospital period. Hospital personnel tended to support the separation of mothers and adult daughters. Perhaps most important, personnel treated these patients as wives and mothers rather than as daughters. This seemed to be true among the patients themselves as well. Thus the obligations of the wives to their mothers were de-emphasized; indeed, the mothers came to *feel* intrusive in this setting. Their rights over their daughters tended to be implicitly challenged, and they were provided a rationale for withdrawal.

The functional alternative to the former triadic pattern provided by hospitalization also had critical consequences for the participation of the husband. It relieved him of the pressures of his wife's dependency as well as of threatening demands for continuous intimacy and full marital responsibility. This freed the husbands of their characteristic need to encourage their wives' involvements with the maternal figure and in this way helped to weaken the mother-daughter interdependency. The revival of affection in the husband and the formation of new resolutions to make a go of the marriage and to attempt to maintain an independent household were closely linked to this change. For example, Mr. Yale's readiness to assume marital family responsibilities was contingent—before, during, and after hospitalization—on the availability of a second center of responsibility—his mother-in-law, the hospital, or, later, a working wife with significant emotional investments outside the home.

The hospitalization tended to draw the husband more closely into a position of involvement and responsibility in another way also. In the final stages of the prehospital crisis, it was the husband who was expected to sign any necessary papers or to make any decisions about hospitalization. Hospital personnel, too, routinely treated him as *the* person who *should be* responsible for his wife. The reciprocal of this induction of the husband into the role of responsible relative was emphasis on the wife's role as *wife*. This social process, too, constituted a pressure away from the earlier pattern in which the husband withdrew to the periphery of the family while mother and daughter came together in symbiotic interdependency and toward a pattern in which husband and wife were more involved with each other and the mother was moved toward the periphery of involvement.

In these ways, hospitalization itself contributed to the disruption of the characteristic triadic patterns and favored a uniform direction of outcome along the lines of a revived marital coalition more independent of the maternal figure. The relative importance of this change, in contrast to formal therapies, cannot be judged from our data, but it is this change which offers the wife a second chance to work out an altered relationship to mother, husband, and children in the posthospital period.

The observed short-term changes in family life proved relatively stable in two of the four cases considered here. After release, Mrs. Low entered into psychotherapy with her husband's encouragement and found in it support for her struggle against the maternal attachment. Simultaneously Mr. Low, for the first time in their marital life, held a job and received promotions. His earlier occupational failures and instability had been an important factor in and justification for continual family dependence on the mother's help. At our last formal follow-up contact, twenty-one months after release, Mrs. Low appeared to be free of psychotic symptoms, and the marital family had retained its relative independence. An informal encounter with this family almost five years after release confirmed this favorable picture.

The Arlens bought a new home shortly after release and moved into it with their children. In a final interview thirteen months after her release, Mrs. Arlen was caring for the home and her children, more satisfied and optimistic than ever before about herself and her marriage and more active and comfortable in social situations than at any previous time. For the first time in her life, she felt able to go out on her own and do family and personal shopping. Mr. Arlen had taken the initiative in setting up the separate household and actively supported his wife's efforts to resist interventions by her mother-in-law. This was in decided contrast to the prehospital period, during most of which the Arlens lived with the husband's mother.[4]

In the other two cases, a partial erosion of the short-term family reorganization took place. Mrs. Karr successfully prodded her husband to buy a home miles from her mother, who had been living next door. Mr. Karr passively acquiesced, but, when his wife began to feel anxious and "weak" shortly after the move, he supported her impulse to sell the home and once again move

---

[4] Mrs. Arlen's mother, who also figured importantly in the case, died suddenly during the hospital period.

next door to her mother. Withal, some two years after release, the Karrs had maintained some increased capacity to manage their own affairs. Her mother seemed less inclined to be continually helpful in an intrusive way, a constraint at least partially linked to a fear that this might cause her daughter to become ill. Mrs. Karr was recurrently troubled with "nervousness," fatigue, and various somatic complaints but had not experienced another psychotic episode.

The Yales began the posthospital period with renewed hopes of increased closeness, independence, and stability. But within a week, Mr. Yale was anxious and irritable and complaining vaguely, without being able to specify any behavior, that his wife was "too dependent" on him. She did not "cling" as she had shortly before hospitalization, nor did she make explicit demands, he said, but somehow she reminded him of his mother from whom he had early struggled to detach himself. Over the next weeks, arguments alternated with what both designated an "armed truce." A few months after release, the couple separated, and Mrs. Yale and her child moved to her mother's home in another city. Later, Mr. Yale moved near his wife, the marital partners were reconciled, and they rented an apartment near her mother. Mrs. Yale was now working and contributing significantly to the support of the family; she also found much emotional gratification in her job. She retained some emotional distance from her mother, more successfully than before. She was free of obvious psychiatric symptoms. This was the situation at the time of the final interview more than two years after her release from the hospital.

We believe that a decisive factor in the stability of the family reorganizations achieved during the hospital period was the support the wife was able to obtain, especially from her husband, in preserving her new position. Mr. Arlen and Mr. Low continued to support the change initiated by hospitalization; Mr. Yale and Mr. Karr were unable to tolerate the demands placed on them by an independent marital family. This impression is consistent with our earlier statement that the crisis of separation is a family as well as an individual task and crisis. It should be added that only Mrs. Low received psychotherapeutic assistance after hospitalization. The therapy clearly helped support the changes the family sought.

Over-all, hospitalization seemed to have disrupted the triadic pattern of accommodation and to have given the participants a second chance to evolve a different set of relationships. This opportunity was limited, however, by the persistent inner and outer forces which shaped the original triadic pattern, and in the posthospital period the participants confronted anew their interlocking problems of living. In these cases, then, hospitalization did not simply repair disorganized people and disordered relationships, restoring the *status quo ante.* Conversely, it did not fundamentally alter the salient life patterns out of which the prehospital crisis arose. The effects of hospitalization were greater than mere restoration and less than radical resolution.

The whole sector of effects described here—which concern the fabric of the patient's life, the persistent pattern of intimate integrations in which he is involved—occurs outside planned and conceptualized diagnosis and therapy. Nonspecific aspects of hospitalization functioned to provide an alternative to the triadic pattern and to draw the husband into a position of somewhat greater involvement and responsibility. The unplanned nature of this effect is emphasized by the following instance in which specific, case-oriented intervention constituted a direct threat to the incipient reorganization of family life.

At the time of release, Mrs. Arlen was in relatively good remission and eager to attempt with her husband to live apart from her mother-in-law and to raise her children without "interference." At the release conference, hospital personnel ventured the recommendation that Mrs. Arlen not assume for some months "full-time care of the children." The recommendation appeared to be based on a general impression that she was anxious about assuming maternal responsibilities and that relatives were available to help her. It was not based on detailed knowledge of prior family patterns

and the intentions of the marital pair. If the recommendation had been followed literally, it is likely that
the former interpersonal triad would have been reconstituted. But the marital partners interpreted the
recommendation in their own way and established a
separate household, calling on Mr. Arlen's mother and
another relative to assist in child care in their own
homes on a temporary day-to-day basis. They soon
disregarded the recommendation entirely.

Thus, the effects of hospitalization we have been considering
are neither planned nor systematically used to further the patient's possibilities of adaptation or therapeutic change. If changes
in family organization are as critical as we believe and as some of
the research cited earlier suggests, then it is important for the
hospital practitioner to widen his conception of the problem he
is asked to treat and consider how he *has* influenced and how he
could influence the decisive intrafamily battles fought just beyond the manifest front of clinical symptomatology.

The relation between changes at the family level and
changes at the individual psychological level is complex and
ambiguous. Clinical improvement ordinarily followed on symp-
tomatic treatment, such as electroshock therapy, rather than on
physical removal from the triadic situation. The clinical improvement, in turn, contributed to the re-establishment of the
marital partner coalition and the separation from the mother. If
we consider, however, the situation near the time of release, we
see that the observed reorganizations had the effect of re-establishing eroded boundaries between the marital and maternal families.
We may reasonably argue that the re-established boundaries provided support for new repressions and variably effective barriers
to the revival of a regressive adaptation.

The fact that these family reorganizations could in any
single instance prove stable warrants comment. John P. Spiegel has
described pathological equilibriums in which "much of what
occurs in the way of behavior is not under the control of any
one person or even a set of persons. . . . Something in the group

process itself takes over as a steering mechanism and brings about results which no one anticipates, or wants, whether consciously or unconsciously."[5] We believe that the prehospital accommodative patterns in these families had become stereotyped in a way that held wife, mother, and husband fixed in processes they were unable to control or modify. These self-regulating pathological systems were disrupted by the psychotic episode itself and substantially modified during hospitalization. The fact that the new family organization could eventually become a relatively stable self-regulating system in which the wife could maintain more satisfactory defensive and adaptive strategies attests to the power of ongoing family structures and affords some hope that breaking up pathological family equilibriums is not quite the same as writing in sand.

The Disengaged

The organization of marital family life around the continuing availability of a maternal figure was infrequent. In most cases the marital partners and their children lived together as a relatively self-contained nuclear family without regular recourse to assistance from a particular third party. In eleven families the marital partners gradually established a relationship based on mutual disengagement, emotional distance, and lack of explicit demands on each other. This development was neither abrupt nor entirely consistent, but the trend of interaction was toward mutual inaccessibility and the construction of separate worlds of involvement. This outcome was invariably preceded by a period of open dissatisfaction with the marriage on the part of one or both partners. Mutual withdrawal functioned as a substitute for open conflict; it also functioned as a substitute for the formal dismemberment of the marital family unit.

In this type of family accommodation, the patterned response to distress on the part of the wife was further withdrawal by the husband, resulting in further disengagement of the marital

[5] John P. Spiegel, "The Resolution of Role Conflict Within the Family," *Psychiatry*, XX (1957), 1–16, 2.

partners. These families suffered an acute crisis when the accommodation became intolerable to one of the partners. In some cases the crisis was initiated by the husband, for example, by the establishment of an extramarital liaison and the decision to seek divorce. In other cases the pattern of mutual withdrawal was disrupted by the wife's increasing agitation, somatic and psychic complaints, and repeated verbal and behavioral communications that she was unable to go on. However the pre-hospital family crisis was initiated and whether it was experienced by the participants as a demand for increased or reduced marital involvement, the change indicated a collapse of the marital adaptation.

We wish to explore now whether the earlier marital equilibrium was restored during or after hospitalization, whether it was modified in some way, and how institutional processes in the mental hospital contributed to observed reorganizations.

The direction of family reorganization in the eleven disengaged cases was not uniform. In three cases, the earlier pattern of mutual withdrawal was confirmed by actual separation, and the wives did not return at release to their original family setting. In three other cases, the wives returned to their original families, but the families had been reorganized in the direction of their further exclusion from meaningful participation. In five cases the wife returned to a marital family in which both partners were making ambivalent, conflicted, but obvious gestures toward reinvolvement and toward creating a basis for a closer marital relationship.

We may thus judge that institutional processes associated with mental hospitalization did not in any simple way determine the direction of these short-term crisis resolutions. We believe that the most critical determinant of these divergent outcomes was the readiness of the husband, and to a lesser degree of the wife, to accept reinvolvement in marital family life. There was, however, an interaction between institutional processes and family reorganization which warrants our attention.

Each of these families experienced two broad crosscurrents promoted by mental hospitalization which provided contrasting opportunities for reorganization. The first current moved toward the permanent exclusion of or withdrawal by the patient from his former community ties. A commonly recognized risk of mental hospitalization, vivid in the consciousness of patients and their families, is that the patient may permanently adapt to an intramural identity and a new life in the institution or that others may adapt to his absence and resist his eventual return. It is significant that we did not have occasion to emphasize this current in discussing the impact of hospitalization on triadic family organizations. This was because the three participants' involvement tended to tie them together rather than to separate them. In the cases now under consideration, the situation was quite different. Withdrawal had been persistently reciprocated by withdrawal, and the prehospital pattern had moved toward the detachment of the wife from family roles. In this situation the psychological barriers which had separated the couple as residents of a single household became physical and social realities in the barrier between the hospitalized wife and the husband in the community. This change afforded new conditions for reinforcing or confirming the exclusion or withdrawal of the wife from her family.

The removal of the wife from the home provided opportunities for a motivated husband to reorganize his life unilaterally in ways that anticipated permanent exclusion. Mr. Baker, for example, began to live with a girl friend and to make definite plans for divorce and eventual remarriage. Mr. Thorne made arrangements for child care and proceeded with plans to sell the family home and move into a small apartment. Mr. Price, as far as we know, never planned divorce or official separation. During hospitalization, however, he continued to personally assume his wife's domestic and child-care functions, further confirming a family organization in which her presence and participation were superfluous. He took no initiative to obtain her release and accepted her eventual return with obvious reluctance. These examples illustrate one obvious way in which hospitalization can further the construction of separate worlds. Hospitalization did not create the disengagement of these husbands but did provide conditions which facilitated exclusion of the wives from their current scheme of living. Further, hospitalization placed the husband in a position which he could use to impede his wife's reintegration into the family. He ordinarily served as her primary source of information about the children and other important ties, and, if he chose not to visit for a time or not to bring the children to visit when his wife was allowed a brief pass, he could in this way contribute to her isolation. The husband had to come to get his wife if she was to go out on pass, and he was responsible for signing her out and vouchsafing her return. Reluctance to do so would confine her immediate life to the ward.

If the husband did use hospitalization to close ranks behind his wife, her opportunities to resist this change were inherently limited and desperate. A rather extreme example is the Price family. Mr. Price was unwilling to convey any interest in his wife's return to hospital personnel, so she forged a letter over his signature to the ward physician stating that she was missed terribly at home, was needed there, and should be released as soon as possible.

The process of further withdrawal by the wife from family life could also find support through hospitalization. From the time of admission, Mrs. White indicated a desire to stay in the hospital. She wore hospital-issue clothing, which was not required, because it made her feel "all in the hospital." She resisted being taken off hospital grounds by her husband for Thanksgiving dinner, declined a pass over the Christmas holidays, and expressed reluctance to see her children. Later she told her husband to discontinue visiting her.

One current promoted by hospitalization, then, reinforced and confirmed the prior pattern of mutual withdrawal. We have already noted, however, that this particular outcome was not the only one observed in these cases. Further, this outcome never came about smoothly, and the impediments which arose were also related to processes initiated by hospitalization. We must recognize a second current associated with hospitalization which moved in the opposite direction.

The second current promoted the re-establishment of family ties through the reciprocal induction of the wife and husband into the roles of mental patient and responsible relative. As this current operated side by side with the other, cross pressures were readily observable when the partners sought to withdraw from each other and the family. The Quinns illustrate this point. Mrs. Quinn's mother and sisters attempted to persuade Mr. Quinn to postpone divorce plans until his wife recovered. When he refused to do so, they wrote to the ward physician to inform him of the husband's plans and to ask his help. The physician agreed that it would be better for the husband to wait. "In general," he said, "it is bad for people to start divorces during the acute illness, since at that time judgment is often bad on the part of both parties." During the initial weeks of hospitalization, Mr. Quinn responded to the inherent claims of the roles of sick wife and concerned husband by concealing from both his wife and hospital personnel his intention to seek divorce. In contacts with the hospital staff he sought confirmation for his view that his wife was hopelessly ill, would never recover, or would recover so partially that she could never be expected to resume responsibilities as wife and mother. When hospital personnel offered a more hopeful prognosis, Mr. Quinn lost faith in their diagnostic competence and attempted to avoid further contact with them.

The wives were also subjected to pressures to retain their marital family involvements. Hospital personnel and other patients assumed that the wife would want to return to her family and consistently treated protestations to the contrary as manifestations of her illness. Mrs. White, whose withdrawal was described above, was gradually but persistently encouraged to return to her family, and her husband was encouraged to ignore her desire that he not visit.

In general, husbands or wives who were attempting to effect a separation experienced cross pressures associated with their roles as responsible relative and mental patient. They would in turn obscure their plans from those who might press them toward greater involvement or censure them, would equivocate for a time, and would minimize contact with each other, with relatives, and with hospital personnel.

When the prehospital family situation had not reached a point where family dismemberment was actively underway, induction into the roles of mental patient and responsible relative brought the marital partners closer together in a relationship dominated by concern about the illness and recovery. The husband would express regrets that he had not "noticed" his wife's illness earlier, would listen to her complaints, would express concern, and would discuss with his wife ways in which their marital lives could be improved. Such explosive marital issues as the husband's lack of interest in the family or the wife's lack of interest in sex might be discussed for the first time in years in the context of concern for the wife's health. Here, hospitalization dramatized the collapse of the former equilibrium, based on mutual withdrawal, and helped reinstate a relationship of concern and perhaps even of overt conflict. This current, then, operated as a disruption of the former pattern of mutual withdrawal, providing conditions under which the partners could re-establish reciprocal expectations compatible with resumption of marital life.

The prehospital trend of family life had moved in all of these cases toward the detachment of the wife from marital family roles. The short-term impact of hospitalization was to disrupt and reverse this trend in five cases, to ambiguously reinforce it in three cases, and to confirm it by the actual separation of the partners in three cases. Quite apart from specific therapies, implicit meanings and characteristics of mental hospitalization provided these diversely motivated couples with pressures and opportunities to work out the various crisis resolutions observed. Longer-term trends in these families, revealed by posthospital developments, emphasize the strength of the disjunctive forces which had led to mutual withdrawal and the limited effect of hospitalization on this pattern.

In three of the five cases in which marital reinvolvement occurred during hospitalization, this reorganization of family life eroded after release. The wife moved and was moved toward disengagement from participation in the family, as in the following example.

> The Whites attempted after hospitalization to "settle down" and "really live like a married couple for the first time." But in a short time earlier discords reappeared, and each partner withdrew into his own concerns. Mrs. White was rehospitalized briefly fifteen months after release and for a period of several months beginning eighteen months after release. At the last follow-up interview, two years after her first release, Mrs. White was again on leave from the state hospital, her husband was involved in an extramarital affair, and the couple agreed on virtually nothing other than that their marriage had disintegrated and was maintained only for the sake of appearances.

In the three cases in which the trend toward exclusion and withdrawal had been reinforced during hospitalization, but without an actual separation (e.g., Mrs. Price), the wife required rehospitalization. Throughout the period of posthospital observation, these wives remained for the most part detached from active participation in family life.

The three cases of formal separation compelled the most fundamental change in prehospital life patterns and thereby the most radical alteration of the earlier conflict situation. This change permitted Mrs. Thorne to begin working for the first time in almost a decade, to get out of the home and away from maternal responsibilities, and to feel less tormented by identifications with a masochistic and inhibited mother. Later she and her husband were reconciled. Mrs. Thorne continued to work full time, using a housekeeper to take care of the children. These shifts were also gratifying to Mr. Thorne, and the marital relationship seemed more harmonious than at any time since the honeymoon a decade earlier. On the other hand, Mrs. Quinn established a regressive adaptation after release. She withdrew into passivity and almost total social isolation, abandoned all responsibility for child care, and became dependent on female relatives.

No rehospitalization nor recurrences of overt psychotic symptoms were observed in the three cases in which separation compelled a radical reorganization of the earlier conflict situation. In spite of the small number of cases involved, this finding invites speculation. We believe that this observation is consistent with the thesis that the psychotic episode in the study group cases arose in the context of a dilemma which had this very general form: these women came to a point at which they felt unable to sustain strivings as wives and mothers or to tolerate the relinquishment of these strivings. If this very gross formulation approximates reality, it may be that one horn of this dilemma was removed when a formal dismemberment of the marital family was effected during hospitalization. This change permitted the women to reorganize their lives either progressively or regressively but in either case removed them from a situation of continuing conflict. We learn from other instances of non-recurrence of symptoms—for example, Mrs. Arlen—that the situation of continuing conflict built into ongoing family structures may be modified in other ways than by dismemberment of the marital family. These speculative considerations require refinement and test in other longitudinal studies of the relationship between family structure and schizophrenic crises.

Over-all, we may conclude that mental hospitalization did not restore the relational *status quo ante* in most of these cases, but favored some reorganization of family life. The prehospital pattern had moved toward exclusion and withdrawal of the wife from active participation in marital family roles. Hospitalization usually furthered this process or reversed it only temporarily until in the posthospital period mutual withdrawal was re-established. In the latter situation, it is important to note that the first hospitalization provided a model of a solution based on the detachment of the wife from the family as a mental patient, a solution which could be, and ordinarily was, used again in time of crisis.

CRISES OF SEPARATION AND IDENTIFICATION

We found it possible to venture a partial account of the psychological meaning of the prehospital crisis for certain cases. We proposed that a group of six women foundered on the task of moving beyond childhood roles in the parental family and relinquishing symbiotic ties to a maternal figure. A group of four women foundered on the task of synthesizing dissociated childhood indentifications in their adult identities, especially those conflicted identifications connected to a crucial turning point in their relation to their mothers. In recent chapters we have not explicitly used this distinction, but have focused instead on family processes which transcended and did not specifically require this level of analysis. We return to our earlier theme by sketching observed crisis resolutions in the two groups of cases.

The four identification cases had established patterns of mutual withdrawal with their husbands before hospitalization. During hospitalization some degree of marital reinvolvement by both partners was achieved. However, their posthospital experiences were uniformly unfavorable. Three cases were rehospitalized; the fourth, Mrs. Mark, was overtly psychotic but lived in the marital family as if in a one-person ward. None of the four maintained a stable remission during the period of observation. Their personal crisis resolution was continued psychosis. At the family level, crisis resolution consisted of unofficial disengagement of the wife from marital family roles and of the partners from each other. None sought divorce; rather, the wife moved and was moved toward chronic patienthood, and the husband organized his life around her exclusion.

The outcomes in the six cases of separation crisis were generally more favorable. Four were in their marital families at the last follow-up, had maintained a stable remission, and were functioning better and more independently than during their prehospital careers. A fifth was in the marital family, intermittently disturbed but apparently not psychotic, and slightly less regressively involved with her mother. The sixth (Price) was in a mental hospital and seemed well on her way toward chronic patienthood.

The difference in outcomes for the two groups is striking; we cannot, however, offer a comprehensive explanation of it. We do not believe that the identification crisis cases would have been rated sicker on a premorbid adjustment scale than their more fortunate counterparts in the other group. The identification crisis cases returned on release to the situations which had mobilized their crises, but it is difficult to conjecture just what external changes could have effectively alleviated their inner conflict. In one case (White) psychotherapy after hospitalization did not alter the progressively downhill course of events.

In the separation cases we have been able to identify and relate changes in family organization to adaptive personal changes. We have seen that separation cases caught up in triadic family patterns were helped by hospitalization to achieve some weakening of the maternal tie. The family reorganizations which took place supported newly reinstituted repressions. When family structures maintained these supports and barriers, the wives were able to function more effectively and independently and to achieve a more adaptive psychic equilibrium.

When separation cases were caught up in mutual withdrawal patterns before hospitalization, as with Mrs. Price and Mrs. Thorne, crisis resolution was somewhat different. Mrs. Thorne was separated from her husband at release, and this seemed to free her from the need for a continuing symbiotic relationship. She lived alone and went to work and in the subsequent marital reconciliation occupied an altered role which did not require her to remain home as a mother and in which she did not turn to others for mothering. This example emphasizes anew that the intense symbiotic need of the wife patient may be closely tied to a particular organization of family life. Mrs. Price returned to a family situation changed only in the direction of her further exclusion and thus drifted into chronic patienthood.

7

Conclusion

Summary and Implications

We have attempted to explore certain links between schizophrenic episodes, the marital family settings in which they occurred, and the institutionalized remedial processes which were brought to bear when personal and family adaptations failed. Specifically, we have described (a) the development in the marital family setting of severe personal crises which eventuated in the wives' schizophrenic disorganization; (b) characteristic accommodations evolved in these families to the future patients' distress, manifest psychiatric symptoms, and withdrawals from role performance; (c) the relationships between such family accommodations and the use of professional resources for the management of mental illness, including hospitalization; and (d) characteristic changes in family organization occurring during hospitalization and afterward, the ways in which hospitalization itself contributed to these changes, and the broad effect of such changes on the personal and social reorganization of the patient's life.

The investigation has been avowedly exploratory. Findings and impressions are based on a very small number of cases. We relied on the "soft" data yielded by semistructured interviewing

117

and observations and on clinical-inductive methods of codification and analysis which are vulnerable to subjective distortions in selection, emphasis, and interpretation. We sought access to certain kinds of information and processes and to certain possibilities of hitting on unforeseen relationships, at the cost of methodological rigor and determinate boundaries of certainty for our findings and generalizations.

It should be recalled that the prehospital period is known to us primarily from retrospective accounts, although in most instances we had access to some records made at the time of contact with social agencies, physicians, and others. Intensive contact with key informants and the simultaneous use of a variety of additional sources provided partial but certainly imperfect protection against the distortions inherent in retrospective accounts.

A most serious methodological problem is that we studied only career lines which eventuated in mental hospitalization. In this sampling situation, it is easy to attribute causation and inevitability to sequential events which are in reality only fortuitously or weakly linked. This is because the investigator does not see similar sequences leading to other than the preselected outcome—in our case, we did not study career lines leading elsewhere than hospitalization. The longitudinal data did make it possible, however, to use patients and families as their own control on some prehospital issues. If, for example, a certain kind of deviant behavior was associated with and cited as a cause for hospitalization but had occurred earlier without this outcome, we could infer that the behavior in itself was not a sufficient cause of hospitalization.

DEVELOPMENT OF CRISES

Clinical schizophrenia is often precipitated when a young person, prompted by inner and outer requirements, attempts to leave home and to function as an adult. This frequent pattern of precipitation has provided one significant point of departure for research about schizophrenia. The nature of the disability which underlies this difficulty of transition into adult life and the early developmental processes in the parental family which may contribute to it have been the subject of much investigation and speculation. Earlier work often focused on the pathogenic characteristics of parents, usually the mother;[1] later investigations have sought to identify pathogenic characteristics of family communication processes or family organization.[2]

Our work with schizophrenic wives supplements the historic emphasis of many of these studies by directing attention to the contemporary vicissitudes of the transition from childhood roles in the parental family to the responsibilities and prerogatives of adult life in a new family of one's own. The women in our study group experienced severe difficulties at such transition points of young adulthood as leaving home, marrying, and becoming parents. We have suggested that for some cases the critical task pressed by participation in the marital family concerned separation, especially from symbiotic ties to a maternal figure. Other cases foundered on the task of synthesizing childhood identifications, especially those revived by becoming like the mother in some frightening and conflicting way. In yet other cases, we did not venture an account of the critical threats mobilized by marital family participation but merely noted the presence of gross conflict in confronting the requirements of these stages of life.

The women did not, however, ordinarily become overtly psychotic in immediate conjunction with these transitions. Even cases with very primitive maternal fixations and pervasive developmental arrest, such as Mrs. Karr, managed for some time

[1] See for example, Trude Tietze, "A Study of Mothers of Schizophrenic Patients," *Psychiatry*, XII (1949), 55–65.

[2] Representative examples of this trend include such articles as those of Gregory Bateson, Don D. Jackson, Jay Haley, and John Weakland, "Toward A Theory of Schizophrenia," *Behavioral Science*, I (1956), 251–264; Bowen, *op. cit.*; Theodore Lidz, Alice Cornelison, Dorothy Terry, and Stephen Fleck, "Intrafamilial Environment of the Schizophrenic Patient. VI The Transmission of Irrationality," *A.M.A. Archives of Neurology and Psychiatry*, LXXIX (1958), 305–316; C. Peter Rosenbaum, "Patient-Family Similarities in Schizophrenia," *Archives of General Psychiatry*, V (1961), 120–126; and Lyman Wynne, Irving Rychoff, Juliana Day, and Stanley Hirsch, "Pseudo-Mutuality in the Family Relations of Schizophrenics," *Psychiatry*, XXI (1958), 205–220. The bibliographies of each of these articles contain valuable references to other important work.

to preserve an adaptation free of manifest psychotic symptoms. Such adaptations depended on, and were conjointly fashioned with, the husbands and other intimates. We identified various family solutions to related conflicts and observed that these accommodations created a precarious equilibrium for the wives, providing neither the opportunity for continued progressive development nor the possibility for simple regressive retreat. The wives thus remained trapped in a somewhat muted but continual conflict until inner and outer circumstances disrupted personal and family patterns of adaptation. Their crises of transition were therefore shaped, on the one hand, by strategic demands pressed by marital family participation as these played on earlier developmental defects and, on the other hand, by the way in which these demands were modified by conjointly fashioned family arrangements.

These observations and impressions suggest the extent to which the specific adult fate of even very severe developmental defects depends critically on the all too typically unspecified environmental factors. These factors, which often derive from the immediate family setting, serve to mobilize conflicts, to require altered adaptations, and to coerce adaptive possibilities in directions which may be more-or-less crippling and dangerous. We have seen that particular family patterns may protect immature women from the ordinary demands of adult life, but such patterns may also become fixed pathological integrations which imprison all the participants in destructive modes of interaction. In a few cases—especially Arlen, Low, and Thorne— the breaking up of a pathological pattern during or after hospitalization permitted family life to move toward a very different and less destructive arrangement. This phenomenon, even in a few instances, lends support to the hope that systematic attention to modifying unfavorable family processes could be a most useful approach in forestalling or ameliorating schizophrenic regressions. It should be remembered that the modifications which took place in these three families were not the result of planned action by treatment personnel. In fact, there are few models for planned rational intervention at this level of action, and innovations in research as well as in treatment are required to develop effective models.

We believe that it would be particularly valuable to study disturbed patients and families in crises similar to those we have described, but to enter the scene at as much earlier a point as possible. The value of this is that the investigator could then directly observe a range of outcomes other than hospitalization, including relatively good outcomes. He could observe restorative as well as disorganizational sequences, family accommodations which tend to limit and reverse pathology rather than merely to ignore or intensify it. The explicit aim should be to learn what factors help a disturbed family to reorganize in ways which support the personal stability of its members. This knowledge would provide the basis for rational models of intervention at the family level, as well as contribute to our limited theoretical understanding of how family structures stabilize the personalities of *adult* members.

OBTAINING PROFESSIONAL HELP

We have seen that the study group wives were grossly disturbed for some time without being defined as mentally ill and without any kind of psychiatric or other professional care. Prior to hospitalization, the wife might have been severely depressed, immobilized, weeping, and withdrawn for weeks or even months; she might be unable to perform even routine duties as a housewife and mother most of the time over several years; she might express bizarre, delusional ideas or even noticeably carry on conversations with unseen people without provoking her husband or other relatives to seek professional care or hospitalization for her. These findings are similar to those of others.[3] Commonly, the schizophrenic patient and his family first come to psychiatric attention during what is experienced as an unmanageable emergency. Prior to this public phase of the crisis and

[3] See for example Yarrow, Schwartz, Murphy, and Deasy, *op. cit.;* also Myers and Roberts, *op. cit.,* pp. 213–220; and Whitmer and Conover, *op. cit.*

often again after it, the disturbance of the patient is in some way managed in a community setting.

Frequently, the relevant community setting is the family, which then serves as the immediate agency of social control, forming a strategic boundary between the individual and more formal means of social control. The family evolves mechanisms for coping with the deviant behavior. Professional help and intervention are sought only when and as family mechanisms of control are experienced as inadequate or inappropriate. In the current climate of mental health attitudes and activities, even extreme accommodative patterns of the family are not ordinarily abandoned until they collapse. It is this collapse which renders the situation unmanageable and ushers in the public phase of the prehospital crisis.

We described two organizations of marital family life which accommodated deviant behavior. We observed how each of these family organizations was disrupted and linked the accommodative pattern and its disruption to recognition of illness, seeking and using professional help, and the circumstances of mental hospitalization.

In one accommodative pattern, the future patient and her husband moved from each other emotionally, effected patterns of uninvolvement, and reciprocated withdrawal by further withdrawal. The patient moved and was moved toward exclusion away from interpersonal ties and from any meaningful links in social reality. This situation was compatible with very high family tolerance for deviant behavior, primarily because deviance was ignored by the husband and not visible to the community. Early entry of the wife into professional treatment was limited by her own withdrawal and by her husband's lack of interest. If the wife did make contact with a psychiatrically oriented helper, the husband, at least initially, experienced this situation simultaneously as of no concern to him and as a potential threat to his own disinvolvement. This accommodation was eventually disrupted by a shift in the husband's or wife's toleration for it. The husband might decide to seek divorce; the wife might express through increasing agitation her inability to go on. In either case hospitalization itself was likely to take place only after the wife's deviance finally came to the attention of the larger community and extrafamily pressure was brought to bear.

In the second accommodative pattern, the wife and a maternal figure became locked in mutual involvement, effected patterns of intense interdependency, and reciprocated withdrawal by concern. The husband ordinarily supported and participated in the establishment of this pattern. The future patient thus moved and was moved toward a bond in which interlocking needs tied the participants together rather than isolated them. This situation was also compatible with high family tolerance for deviant behavior, primarily because the deviance had become a necessary component of family integration. This accommodative pattern did not simply make outside help superfluous for a while; more to the point, outside help would have constituted a threat to the mother-daughter interdependency, carrying the implication that it was inadequate or unnecessary or even harmful. It was the collapse of this accommodative pattern which led to the wife's contact with physician or psychiatrist. The collapse occurred when the wife was unable to tolerate continuing maternal assistance at a time when no other comparable support was available to her. This circumstance for seeking outside help is analogous to that characterized by Kalis and her colleagues as "bind with previous helper."[4] Hospitalization itself came about after the wife had come to feel simultaneously alienated from both mother and husband. She then pressed for physical removal from the conflict situation.

One important consequence of these accommodative patterns was that the wife did not become accessible to outside help or treatment in many instances until her psychosis was well advanced. By then her capacity to use help was minimal. Her need was so urgent, her control of impulses and assessment of reality so impaired, her distrust so intense, that any intervention short

[4] Betty Kalis, Robert Harris, Rodney Prestwood, and Edith H. Freeman, "Precipitating Stress as a Focus in Psychotherapy," *Archives of General Psychiatry,* V (1961), 219–226.

of hospitalization was too little and too late. A second consequence of these patterns was that other family members had to
endure in their homes the presence of a grossly disturbed and sometimes psychotic person for very extended times. We are unable to
assess the impact of this experience on the children, as we did not
systematically interview or observe them but focused on children
primarily as sources of gratification and threat to adult family
members. The case histories we have presented provide at least
a glimpse of what the husbands and children encountered and of
the chaotic circumstances in which they lived, sometimes for long
periods.

Family accommodation patterns sometimes permit a psychiatric crisis to be contained and then resolved without recourse
to outside assistance and without unfavorable consequences. But
when difficulties persist for an extended period and the family
adapts to deviance as a routine part of family life, the delay in
seeking remedial help is undoubtedly costly to the prepatient
and to other family members as well.

There have not been, however, very many alternative treatments to mental hospitalization, especially for those with limited
financial means. There has been a large gap between the total
institutional care provided by the mental hospital on the one
hand and the limited contact and protection provided by once-
a-week outpatient psychotherapy on the other.[5] In many study
group families, the patient and husband thought of hospitalization as a virtually permanent step, yet no other alternatives were
visible to them. From this perspective, denial of deviance and
accommodation to it are alternatives to what would be experienced as the irreversible disaster of hospitalization. The development of day hospitals, night hospitals, acute treatment
centers in community hospitals, and community mental health
centers are gradually making alternatives to removal and isolation of the deviant more visible to more people. At the same
time, the image of the large mental hospital as a permanent
custodial setting is changing in slow response to the real changes

---

[5] Sampson, Ross, Engle, and Livson, *op. cit.*

taking place in the orientation and effectiveness of these institutions. These changes will undoubtedly modify the tendency of some families to accommodate extreme deviance over long periods and will increase their readiness to seek help. Some barriers to earlier detection and treatment may be expected to decline steadily in response to improved and more flexible mental health services.

Some, but perhaps not all. There are study group families in which the passivity and social withdrawal of the prepatient and the husband would greatly delay any step toward help which required action in reality and responsibility for a decision. Such families would be correspondingly difficult to help even if their need was identified. In triadic families, the mother will help her disturbed daughter and simultaneously insulate her from outside help. If the young woman does seek help, she will be burdened not only by intense guilt, but quite possibly by the active interference of her mother, and she can expect little effective support from her husband. In extreme symbiotic situations, it seems unlikely that the young woman would be able to seek help prior to a psychotic crisis. In less extreme symbiotic cases, the person may be able to seek help, but a treatment approach which takes into account the entire family will often be essential. More generally, we must conclude from our work that it will frequently remain difficult to discover—and, more importantly, to be able to provide meaningful early help for—a potential schizophrenic crisis even when the range of community mental health activities broadens. This conclusion is supported by the long-standing nature of manifest illness in many cases.

IMPACT OF HOSPITALIZATION

The mental hospital directed its explicit diagnostic and treatment activity toward the patient and her gross symptoms. Implicitly, the hospitalization constituted a diagnosis and treatment of the family crisis as well. Hospitalization legitimated the removal of the patient from her family, established new conditions of interaction between her and family members, and contributed to the definition of their roles as mental patient and responsible relative. These processes could contribute to the re-establishment of ties between the patient and her intimates; conversely, they could support her permanent exclusion or withdrawal from former community ties. It is easy to selectively observe and emphasize only one side of this dual potentiality and to represent the mental hospital as either the principal cause of or principal cure for the patient's alientation. We found that both alienative and restorative currents are promoted by mental hospitalization and sought to describe the ways in which patients and families utilized hospitalization for re-engagment or further disengagement.

When the prehospital family pattern was characterized by a symbiotic interdependency between the wife and her mother, with the husband at the periphery of this triad, hospitalization supported changes in the direction of a new husband and wife coalition which moved her mother toward the periphery. The transfer of responsibility for the care of the wife to the mental hospital provided a functional alternative to the prior symbiosis. This functional alternative made it easier for both mothers and daughters to disengage themselves a bit and also reduced the husbands' needs to turn their wives' dependency toward their mothers. The role prescriptions for the wife as a mental patient, the husband as the responsible relative, and the mother as a less central figure also supported the realignment of the triad.

When the prehospital family pattern was characterized by reciprocal withdrawal patterns, hospitalization did not have a uniform effect. Hospitalization provided opportunities for either further disengagement of the partners or reconciliation. The most critical determinant of the outcome seemed to be the readiness of the husband, and to a lesser extent of the wife, to accept reinvolvement in marital family life. There was, however, an interaction between institutional processes and family reorganization. Let us consider as an example the process we have designated as the reciprocal induction of the wife and husband into the roles of mental patient and responsible relative. When either partner was attempting to leave the marital relationship, this process operated to impede and complicate the carrying out of that intention. If, however, the motivation to leave was flunctuating or inconsistent, this process operated as a force toward at least temporary reconciliation. It is interesting to note again that the same process had another effect on the prehospital triadic pattern. In the latter instance, it reinforced the husband-wife coalition and limited the immediate power and position of her mother.

Family reorganizations achieved during the hospital period often afforded the marital partners a kind of second chance to better their relationship. This opportunity was limited, however, by the persistent intrapsychic and interpersonal forces which shaped the original patterns. The tentative reorganizations were frequently undone in the weeks or months following the patient's release. But in some instances hospitalization disrupted stereotyped pathological integrations and permitted more constructive patterns to evolve and become stable. In other instances the disruption of prior patterns led only to a more regressive way of life for the patient.

The links proposed between institutional processes and family patterns are plausible, but they are derived after the fact and from observations on very few cases. We believe they warrant further study as hypotheses about important, neglected, and minimally conceptualized processes.

The significance of the longitudinal emphasis employed in this work becomes particularly obvious as we describe the impact of hospitalization on these families or characterize their posthospital patterns of adaptation. The two prehospital accommodations posed distinctly contrasting problems for the hospital period —in the one case, the problem of chronic reciprocal disinvolvement between the patient and her interpersonal community; in the other, chronic reciprocal overinvolvement between the patient and a family member. Further, the (approximately) same institutional processes had demonstrably different results for different pre-existing relational patterns. Family patterns in the posthospital period are not created fresh out of the special status of ex-patienthood or the simple fact of mental hospitalization.

They are, as we have shown, the products of long-term trends modified during the hospital period.

An important general feature of the prehospital trend in most cases was the increasing isolation of the wife from family and social relationships, her more-or-less progressive detachment from participation in social reality. The isolation had different psychological and interpersonal causes in different cases, but, superimposed on these special factors, was the common establishment of a vicious circle of reciprocated withdrawal or intensified symbiosis. It became almost impossible for the patient or other family members to break up the patterns which isolated her, and at the same time these patterns insulated her from corrective influences of the larger community. We mean by corrective influences not only or even primarily therapeutic activities, but the ordinary run of support, gratification, structure, and reality-testing afforded by encounters with others. We do not have any practical answer to the problems posed by these vicious circles of isolation and insulation, but we are suggesting that the difficulty is not only in the disease process or the psychodynamics of the patient, but also in reactions of the individual, the family, and the community to the deviance of mental illness. These reactions constitute one side of and help to perpetuate the vicious circles.

Cumming and Cumming have hypothesized that the traditional social response to mental illness is, first, denial of deviance; then, when denial is no longer possible, the physical and social isolation of the deviant; and, finally, insulation of the problem.[6] One side of this coin is the reaction of the individual patient and his family to deviance—a reaction which may lead to a vicious circle of increasing isolation within the family, either in the form of autistic loneliness or of symbiotic relatedness. The other side of the coin is the traditional custodially oriented mental hospital functioning as an insular, semiautonomous province, physically and socially separated from its community and minimally con-

[6] Elaine Cumming and John Cumming, *Closed Ranks* (Cambridge, Mass.: Harvard University Press, 1957).

cerned with the extramural history and world of its inmates. The consequences of this pattern are still obvious even in as progressive and enlightened a state mental hospital as the one we studied. Its patients still ordinarily come to it only at the end of an extended process of personal and family disorganization which has called forth increasingly extreme and disruptive emergency reactions. The hospital is presented for the most part with emergency situations which it must handle as such. The role of the hospital does not include a mandate to reach into the community and to attempt to prevent such emergencies from arising, and, inevitably enough, the interest of its staff in the long sweep of the prehospital crisis or in the family setting in which it arose is more academic than practical. They are right; such concerns have no immediate therapeutic payoff in their hospital setting. We have seen, however, that in some cases—for example, the Arlens—the lack of knowledge of important family issues can lead to useless or inappropriate recommendations. More broadly, we have argued that the mental hospital *is* influencing family processes which have a bearing on the patient's recovery and future stability and that it would indeed be practical to observe these influences and to conceptualize them explicitly. The paucity of knowledge of these processes is part of the heritage of the isolation-denial-insulation pattern and at the same time helps to perpetuate it.

The large mental hospital has been changing for many years. In addition, efforts are being undertaken in many places to provide a range of alternatives between no treatment or limited treatment by outpatient psychotherapy in an office setting and total institutional care. For example, day-care centers provide supervision, protection, support, and some treatment for a patient during the time when a working relative cannot be with him. This arrangement leaves the patient in the family and community without placing as severe a burden on family members as the kinds of accommodations we described. The day-care center may also provide direct stimulation to counter the pattern of increasing isolation. The night hospital permits a patient to hold a job in the community by day and yet return to a struc-

tured, supervised, protected environment at night. Acute treatment wards in general hospitals permit the patient to be treated
nearer home, quite possibly with a much briefer inpatient stay
and with less social stigma. Community mental health centers
may provide all of these services (day care, night hospital, acute
treatment inpatient service) and in addition offer outpatient
psychotherapy, child guidance, family therapy, consultation, and
a variety of more specialized services. The existence of a range of
alternatives will free the professional worker as well as the patient from all-or-none choices and compel serious attention to
individual and family needs. These and other changes in psychiatric care are the opening wedge of a breach in the denial-isola-
tion-insulation pattern. The disruption of this pattern will make
it both possible and necessary to come to understand the full
course of psychiatric crises rather than only that fragment which
now comes to public attention. In particular, it will become both
necessary and possible to better understand how family processes
affect the stability and instability of the adult personality.

Appendix

Case Studies

Case materials are widely used (and widely scattered) throughout this book as illustrations of particular patterns or processes rather than as individual case studies. The reader may find short case summaries useful in their own right as well as for background about various themes developed by the authors. These summaries may also allow the reader to form an independent perspective about the experiences of the women in the study group.

In addition to using code names, we have freely altered identifying data to safeguard the confidentiality of the patients and their husbands. The information here may thus differ slightly on some points from the statistical summary of actual study group characteristics presented in Chapter 1.

SHIRLEY ARLEN

The Arlens had been married only two years when Shirley was hospitalized. Shirley was twenty-six, and her husband James was twenty-four. They had two infant sons, nineteen and five months old. Shirley was herself the fifth of eight children born

131

to a poor urban family. Her father was a passive and dependent man who rarely intervened in family affairs; her mother was an energetic woman who ran the family but was a very casual housekeeper and lax disciplinarian. Her mother expected and demanded little of Shirley. Shirley did little housework and was never assigned domestic responsibilities. Shirley's mother bought Shirley's clothes for her into adulthood and did not seem to mind Shirley's passivity and withdrawal. Shirley was a shy, sweet, indrawn girl who remained for the most part in the family circle. She disliked school, felt terribly self-conscious, and would feign sickness in order to be absent when she had to recite. After she was old enough to quit school, Shirley held several unskilled jobs for brief periods. She would quit jobs or become sick and be absent from work until dismissed. When boys began to approach her during adolescence, she was passively compliant, accepted their sexual overtures, and would continue the relationship until the boy decided to drop her. One of the boys she met seemed very nice, and she liked him a great deal, but he made it clear that he did not want to marry her. At about this time she met James, began to go with him, and discovered she was pregnant. She suspected that her other boy friend was the father, but he had rejected her, and James was interested in marriage.

From the beginning of the marriage, Shirley felt overwhelmed by the responsibilities she had assumed. She could not spend money because it did not really belong to her. She had never shopped for groceries or clothes and could not do so now. She did not feel able to decide what to cook and felt uneasy in preparing meals. She felt that James was critical of what she did do and that he always compared her unfavorably to his dominating mother to whom he was so obviously attached. Even routine housework seemed more than she could manage. The Arlens moved in with his parents prior to the birth of the first child. Shirley's mother-in-law was a managing, intrusive woman, and she quickly took over the child as if it were her own. Shirley felt thoroughly intimidated and withdrew further. Shirley soon became pregnant again, and she and James decided to move into a separate household. Shirley was eager to be on her own and to try to take charge, but once again the responsibilities proved frightening. James himself took over the household chores, and Shirley felt increasingly guilty. She became lax in caring for her child, leaving him in bed for most of the day and rarely playing with him. After the birth of her second child, Shirley spent much time in bed and asked James to take the older child to his mother's house each day. Shirley began to see a psychiatrist for psychotherapeutic help and also asked her mother to come over during the days to provide help with the baby. When her mother was no longer able to come, Shirley had her mother take the newborn son to the parental home and care for him. A few days later Shirley, too, moved to her mother's house, and James moved back to his mother. A week later Shirley entered the hospital because she feared she was losing her mind and might harm someone.

Shirley was hospitalized for thirty-six weeks and received electroshock therapy. Shortly after she was released, the Arlens bought a new home and moved into it with their children. In a final interview thirteen months after release, Mrs. Arlen was caring for her home and children without outside help, was more satisfied and optimistic about herself and her marriage than ever before, and was more socially active and comfortable than at any time in her life. For the first time she felt able to go out on her own and do family and personal shopping. She felt she had begun to grow up.

JOAN BAKER

At the time of hospitalization, Joan Baker was thirty-five, and her husband Arnold forty-one. They had been married for fifteen years and had two daughters, twelve and seven. Joan was born in England and lived there until after her wartime marriage to Arnold, who was then an American soldier. The oldest of three children, Joan had two younger brothers. Her dominating memories and preoccupations about childhood concerned repeated depreciation and rejection by her father. She later learned that her parents had married just before her birth, and she then assumed that her father resented her because she was the cause of his having to marry her mother. However, she characterized her parents' marriage as a congenial one. We know that the parental marriage remained intact, that Joan was raised in one house, and that her father was regularly employed at a good job.

At sixteen Joan quit school and began to work. Three years later she met Arnold shortly after she moved away from home for the first time, to work in a war plant. She said of the courtship, "He was the first good thing that happened to me. He was good to me like my mother." Right after their marriage, however, Arnold became severely asthmatic and was shipped back to a hospital in the United States. Shortly after Joan joined him and became pregnant, Arnold began an affair with another woman and talked of leaving Joan. When the other woman rejected Arnold, Joan accepted him back because "I felt so desperate." Also, she had just learned that one of her brothers had been killed in the war and that her mother had reacted to this news with severe depression as well as physical illness.

Throughout the marriage Arnold rejected and depreciated Joan, and she very often felt left out, worthless, and unloved. She would neglect the housework, daydream about the past, become depressed, and overeat. She became obese. At other times she managed the housework well, dieted strenuously, and was quite socially active with other women. For two or three years before hospitalization, however, Joan was almost chronically depressed. Her husband's older brother, to whom Arnold was very close and with whom he did everything, came to live with them, so once again Joan felt left out. For this or other undetermined reasons, Joan found it hard to be pleasant to anyone, hated herself, overate, and became fat. Her husband had often threatened to leave her during their arguments, and she feared that it might happen. Occasionally she would visit the grounds of a nearby state hospital and watch the patients, explaining to her husband, "I must feel like some of them. I'm lonely and depressed, and I have to go somewhere."

Arnold's brother died rather suddenly, and, after a period of grief and withdrawal, Arnold met a woman at a party and went home with her, leaving Joan on her own. The next day Arnold and Joan quarreled violently, and Arnold said he was going to leave her and live with the other woman. Joan felt very angry and very frightened, threatened violence toward herself or her husband or children, and urged a friend and then her physician to hospitalize her. There is a hospital notation that Mrs. Baker had been hearing voices for a long time, mostly her parents "calling me lots of dirty things." She was diagnosed as schizophrenic reaction, schizo-affective. The research interviewer, who first saw Mrs. Baker immediately after her admission, observed her agitation and depression but did not at any time see or obtain evidence of hallucinations, delusions, or gross psychotic symptoms.

Joan was initially treated with mild doses of tranquilizers, but on a home visit a month after admission she quarreled with her husband about his girl friend and superficially slashed her wrists. She was returned to the hospital and received electroshock therapy. Eighteen weeks after admission she was placed on indefinite leave, ostensibly to her husband. (Joan and Arnold told the hospital that they were reconciled.) She was actually entirely on her own at release, as her husband continued to live with the other woman. We have follow-up information on Mrs. Baker for more than two years after release. She had been working regularly, taking care of one daughter (the other was with her husband), and was seriously involved in a relationship with a man who wanted to marry her. She had felt depressed at times, but never severely.

IRENE JAMES

Irene James was forty at the time of her hospitalization; her husband Ralph was forty-six. They had been married for nine years and had a seven-year-old daughter. It was Irene's second and Ralph's first marriage.

Irene was the youngest of six children. She can remember a period in early childhood when she was very much afraid to be alone and used to climb into bed with her mother, but Irene was less than five when her mother became ill with a bad heart. For about a year her mother was bedridden. She died at the age of forty. Irene thought that overwork in caring for the children had killed her. After the mother's death the family broke up. Irene lived in a series of foster homes, sometimes with the brother

nearest her in age and sometimes alone. Irene always got along
well with her foster parents. She was a good student in school
and a sweet, compliant, inhibited, and nervous girl. Her father
remained near Irene and her brother and visited them regularly.
He established a home for the three of them during Irene's early
teens, and they lived together until his death when she was
twenty-one. While living with her father and brother, she had a
period of marked "nervousness," but we know nothing else about
it.

   After graduation from high school Irene worked and continued to do so until her first marriage at twenty-two. She gave
birth to a daughter a year later. The birth was difficult, and Irene
was ill during and right after pregnancy; she feared dying. Irene
described her first marriage as neither happy nor conflictful—she
and her husband were simply too young, they had very little in
common, and they drifted apart. She sought divorce, and he
agreed amicably; his mother consented to take care of the child.
When Irene decided to divorce her husband and give up her
child, the daughter was five, Irene's own age when her mother
died.

   Irene married Ralph when she was thirty. A reserved, sedate,
conscientious man in his mid-thirties, Ralph had had very little
to do with women and had not really expected to marry. The
Jameses took Irene's daughter to live with them and two years
later had a daughter of their own. Irene felt quite weakened by
childbirth and required substantial help from Ralph in caring
for the baby during its first year. They moved near Ralph's job
so he could spend more time at home. Our impression is that at
this time Irene experienced a self-contained emotional crisis precipitated by identifications with her own mother. Further trouble
developed when Irene was thirty-five, her mother's age when she
was born. Irene experienced severe abdominal pains and menstrual irregularities. She left the Catholic church, fearing that its
teachings about divorce and sin would disturb the younger
daughter and perhaps "split the family apart." Soon after this
Irene became involved in a series of squabbles with neighbors;
this led to a decision to move. During her psychosis several years
later, she interpreted the squabbles as part of a neighbor's com-

plex plot to seduce her. It is not known whether she thought this at the time, but sexual fantasies might have been evoked by the onset of menses in the older daughter. In any event, this daughter chose to go to live with her father right after Irene's difficulties with the neighbors, and Irene's symptoms abated for several years.

Irene's episode began dramatically within a week of her fortieth birthday, which was her mother's age at the time of illness and death. Irene fainted, attributed this to menstrual difficulties, and became convinced that she was entering the change of life. She experienced several events which she interpreted as snubs by neighbors and which she related to the earlier quarrels as part of the seduction plot. She could not distract herself from preoccupations about the plot to break up her family, was unable to do her work, to respond to others, or to sleep. After hospitalization she spoke of plots to make people sick and break up families, she noted the frequency of heart attacks at forty, and she had a reassuring dream in which her mother appeared and told her that doctors now have ways of curing illnesses that used to be fatal.

Irene was released in partial remission after fifteen weeks of hospitalization. She still believed in the reality of the strange neighborhood events but was no longer preoccupied, could keep her ideas to herself, and felt cheerful again. After a few weeks she began to feel very weak and felt as though she was slipping back. A doctor gave her vitamin shots, and she improved dramatically for about a month. She then relapsed into a very withdrawn and autistic state with rambling paranoid delusions. She remained at home in this condition for well over a year. At the end of the twenty-seven months following her first release, she was in the hospital, had been rehospitalized twice, and was overtly psychotic.

WANDA KARR

At the time of hospitalization Wanda Karr was twenty-nine, and her husband Richard was twenty-eight. They had been married for a little over three years and had two daughters. The older daughter was two; the younger had been born about two weeks before.

Wanda's parents were poor, uneducated rural people. She was the middle of three children born of her parents' first marriage. Her older brother was an emotionally disturbed mental defective, but he was kept at home until his parents divorced and was then institutionalized. Wanda's younger brother was killed in an automobile accident shortly after her marriage. The parents were divorced when Wanda was about eleven; she recalls that each had been "running around" for a year or two before the divorce. Her mother remarried almost immediately and moved with her new husband and the two younger children to California. A half sister was born when Wanda was fourteen.

Wanda was an intellectually limited girl and was always considered weak and sickly. Her mother was a domineering, complaining, and inconsistently incorporative woman. For a time she would manage every detail of Wanda's life and then suddenly withdraw with the onset of some self-concern or somatic symptom. Wanda's mother characterized the world outside of the family as hostile and threatening, and she actively discouraged Wanda's few faltering efforts to establish outside interests and relationships and generally encouraged withdrawal into passivity, physical sickness, and helplessness. Wanda made poor progress in school not only because of her limited intellect, but also because of repeated absences owing to nausea or headaches. Her mother never urged her to return. Wanda had few social contacts, dated boys only in fantasy, and never held a steady job.

At twenty-five Wanda met Richard Karr and after a brief courtship married "the only boy I ever really went with." Her mother explicitly opposed the marriage. Although Wanda felt ill on her wedding day, she went through with the ceremony and moved away from mother for the first time. A little later the Karrs accepted financial help from her mother and purchased the house next door. Soon the families had merged under the management of Wanda's mother. The presence of the first child intensified the need of wife, husband, and mother for this kind of interdependency, but it also increased conflicts. Wanda's mother assumed control of the baby, and, when the child learned to talk, she called both mother and grandmother "Mama." During Wanda's second pregnancy she felt even more tired and nervous than she had during the first. Again Wanda regressed, her mother took over, and Wanda regressed further. But Wanda was determined that she was going to nurse her second child (she had felt unable to nurse the first) and began to do so successfully in the hospital. When she came home, however, her tension increased, and she could neither nurse nor relinquish the striving to do so. Her mother encouraged her to stop trying; Wanda responded by drinking large quantities of water. During this period Wanda's mother moved into Wanda's house; Richard stayed next door with Wanda's stepfather and half sister. Wanda's effort to mother her new baby failed, and Wanda succumbed to being helpless and mothered. She became slovenly and withdrawn, then began to violently accuse mother of cruelty and Richard of infidelity. She also feared that she had irreparably harmed the baby and could not be dissuaded from this belief.

Wanda was hospitalized for about eight weeks and received electroshock therapy. She improved and with her family's acquiescence decided not to return from a pass. Wanda prodded her husband into buying a home miles from her mother, but, when she began to feel anxious and weak shortly after the move, Richard supported her impulse to sell the home and once again move next door to her mother. In the two years following release, Mrs. Karr was recurrently troubled with "nervousness," weakness, exhaustion, and various somatic complaints, but she had not experienced another psychotic episode or required rehospitalization, and the Karr family had developed a slightly increased capacity to manage its own affairs.

EVE LOW

Eve and Chester Low were both thirty-eight years old and had been married twelve years at the time of Eve's hospitalization. They had three children—a girl of ten, a boy of seven, and a girl just two. Eve was herself the third of four children. Throughout Eve's childhood her parents were often separated,

and her mother accounted for the separations by the father's inability to provide adequately for his family. During separations
the mother and children would move into the maternal grandmother's home, and the mother would work as a nurse. Eve recalled a period of early closeness to her father and remembered
that her mother disapproved of her sitting on her father's lap.
Early separations from her father were distressing for Eve, and she
was particularly upset when her grandmother downgraded him
for being lazy and inadequate.

Eve's older brother and sister were rebellious in adolescence,
and each got into real trouble. By contrast, Eve was a very good
student and an obedient, inhibited, and very nervous girl. At
this time her mother seemed to become intensely involved with
Eve. She strictly controlled Eve's limited dating, supervised her
clothing and appearance, and made plans for Eve's schooling,
deciding that Eve also should become a nurse. When Eve became interested in a boy and wanted to follow him to college, her
mother insisted that she go to a girl's college instead. For the
most part Eve complied with her mother's wishes and plans. She
became a nurse. She rejected her few suitors. She was very apprehensive about sex and was generally anxious.

Eve's father, with whom she had had very little contact since
childhood, died when she was twenty-five. A few months later she
met Chester Low while on a train en route home to visit her
mother, and she became engaged to marry him during the trip.
Her mother objected, but Eve went ahead with the marriage a
month later. Eve soon began to doubt her love for Chester and
abruptly left him and returned to her mother. Chester followed
her a little later, and their marital relationship resumed. At
times they established an independent household, but Chester
could not hold jobs for long and Eve was often unwell, so they
frequently turned to mother for help. Eve's mother lived with
them and intermittently assumed most of the responsibility for
the house and children when Eve had to work or felt sick or
exhausted. The mother repeatedly berated Chester as a poor provider who did not know the value of money, as a man who
could not do anything really well, as a stubborn misfit, and as a

philanderer. Eve was chronically anxious, somatically preoccupied, guilty, and sexually apprehensive. She often took medication to help her sleep or to calm herself. After the birth of her
third child, in the midst of further marital difficulties and financial chaos, she feared she would lose her mind and sought psychiatric help. The psychiatrist urged her to ask her mother to leave,
and she did so, but her condition worsened, and she withdrew
further from her husband. The psychiatrist moved away and
transferred Eve to a new person. At this point Eve became
acutely psychotic. One symptom was violent repudiation of her
mother.

Eve was hospitalized for eleven weeks and received three
electroshock therapy treatments. She was released in good remission and returned to her husband. She was determined to
stay with him, and Chester, for his part, also seemed more committed to the marriage. Eve entered into psychotherapy with her
husband's encouragement and felt strengthened by it. Simultaneously Mr. Low, for the first time since marriage, held a job
and received promotions. At our last interview, twenty-one
months after release, Mrs. Low appeared free of psychotic symptoms and relatively content. Mr. Low was doing well in his work,
and the marital family had retained its integrity and independence. An informal encounter with this family almost five years
after release confirmed this favorable picture.

JUNE MARK

At the time of hospitalization June Mark was thirty-three,
and her husband Paul was thirty-four. They had been married
twelve years; it was her second marriage and Paul's first. Their
three daughters were eleven, eight, and four. June was herself the
youngest of three girls; her oldest sister was a child of her
father's previous marriage. Her mother belonged to a wealthy,
prominent family in the community. By contrast, her father was
an unskilled laborer, illiterate and poor.

Her mother became ill during the pregnancy with June. Her
illness gradually progressed, and, when June was four, she died.
June's main memories of her mother are of climbing into the in-

valid's bed and being loved and caressed. "That's all I had of my mother." June retained an idealized, almost saintly image of her mother—generous, religious, universally loved. Conversely, she retained an unfavorable image of the maternal aunts who cared for her immediately following mother's death; she remembered them as cruel, stingy (toward her) in spite of their wealth, and ridiculing—they treated her as a shabby little orphan and denied her even the necessities of life. Several months later June's father took his children with him as he traveled about the country and worked at one job and then another. The children were cared for by a series of housekeepers while the father worked. Their economic situation was marginal.

At seventeen June married a boy she met in high school. He was the son of a close-knit, well-to-do family. June diligently sought her mother-in-law's approval and love but was never fully accepted into the family. The marriage foundered, and the couple separated. June met Paul Mark during the trial separation, obtained a divorce, and married for the second time. Unlike June's first husband Paul was a poor boy, the son of migrant farm laborers. He, too, had suffered from maternal abandonment and deprivation during childhood. June and Paul viewed themselves as motherless, abused children who would nurture each other; they referred to themselves as "us kids." Their marriage was very close at first, and later neither could tolerate open feelings of criticism and resentment toward the other. Over the years, however, Paul spent much time away from home in quasi-occupational activities, and June became increasingly absorbed in her children. Also, since childhood June had felt scorned as an impoverished orphan, and from early in her marriage there was some friction with neighbors who supposedly depreciated June's poor furniture and other belongings.

June's problems intensified after the birth of her third daughter, even as her mother's fatal illness had begun with the birth of June, the third girl in the family. June began to neglect the housework and to turn noticeably from her husband to her children. She also felt a little weak; her body did not seem quite right; pregnancy had taken something out of her—even her hair had become lifeless. Later, some months before hospitalization, June became concerned with the cruel and ridiculing attitude of some jealous, wealthy women, fellow members of a community club, toward her daughters. She became so involved with the children that she failed to come home from outings with them to fix dinner for her husband, and she interrupted sexual relations to discuss the children's difficulties with the cruel, wealthy ladies. Despite the family's shaky financial situation, June bought extravagantly expensive gifts for the children. During much of this period Paul spent several nights a week out on a second job. June began to imagine that her neighbors were spreading gossip that she was sexually promiscuous and unfaithful or that her husband was untrue to her. June was hospitalized when her youngest daughter was four, her own age at the time of her mother's death.

June was hospitalized for twelve weeks and received electroshock therapy. She was released in partial remission. Her symptoms worsened about a month later, and she received medication and supportive therapy from a private psychiatrist. Still later, when her condition again grew worse, the psychiatrist gave her outpatient electroshock therapy. She improved, but only for a short time. When last seen, about two years after release, Mrs. Mark was living at home and had not been rehospitalized; she was delusional and had been intermittently psychotic throughout the posthospital period. She was no longer responsible for the household or child care, and her husband no longer tried to relate to her.

JOYCE NOON

At the time of her hospitalization, Joyce Noon was twenty-six, and her husband Mel was thirty-seven. They had been legally married for only two years but had been living together—with occasional separations—for eight years. Their only child, a son, was seven.

Joyce was herself the sixth of nine children. Her early life was chaotic. There was constant parental bickering, many moves, and, most likely, exposure to the sexual stimulation of illicit affairs by older brothers and sisters and perhaps also her parents. Her father left the family when Joyce was eight, and shortly thereafter her mother placed the five youngest children in an orphanage. Later the father returned and removed the children from the orphanage. Over the next several years Joyce lived intermittently with her father, with both parents, in a Catholic home for delinquent girls, with her mother, and with a married older sister. At the time she met Mel Noon, Joyce was eighteen and living with a man. Mel had recently been discharged from the service following a psychiatric breakdown. He was a markedly unstable man with a history of poorly controlled behavior, repeated job changes, and transient relations with women. He had been married twice.

The Noons established a common-law relationship soon after meeting, and their only child, a son, was born about a year later. The Noons remained together in chaotic fashion for eight years, but there were repeated instances of infidelity and abandonment on each side. Joyce is reported to have run off with other men on a number of occasions. At one point Joyce and Mel agreed to separate, and Joyce went to live with her mother. She met and married another man, but this marriage lasted barely a month, and soon Joyce and Mel were again living together. They were formally married when Joyce was twenty-four. For a long time both before and after her marriage, Joyce was involved in an affair she felt unable to terminate, an affair with the husband of the older sister with whom she had stayed in childhood.

About six months before Joyce developed hallucinations, her boy was badly hurt in an accident, and, in circumstances that are not entirely clear, the affair with her sister's husband stopped. Joyce was very worried about the boy; it is also likely that she was experiencing great guilt over the affair with her brother-in-law. She ate very little and began to lose weight. She felt depressed and cried a lot. The voices began, and they taunted her as a whore; they reported that other women were stealing her husband and accused her of stealing other men. She saw her physician, but she did not disclose the hallucinations. He gave her vitamins and reassurance. After several months she felt she could not go on and was hospitalized at her own request.

Joyce was hospitalized for seven weeks, received no electro-shock therapy, and was placed on indefinite leave. We have follow-up information for thirty-three months following first release; during this period she was rehospitalized six times and was in the hospital at the time of our last contact.

LOUISE OREN

Louise Oren was thirty, and her husband Jack was thirty-two at the time of her admission to the state mental hospital. They had been married for nine years and had two children. The older child, eleven, was Louise's illegitimate son, but he had been formally adopted by Jack. The other child was a three-year-old daughter.

Louise was the only child of her mother's third and her father's only marriage, but her mother had had eleven other children by former husbands. Several older brothers and sisters were in the home at times during her childhood. The family had a notable history of illness and death, and a number of children died before Mrs. Oren had become an adult. Mrs. Oren's mother was constantly occupied with making a living to support her family; when home she was a perfectionist as a housekeeper and a rather strict woman who neither smoked nor drank. Her father was an erratically affectionate, hard-drinking, profane man who was an irresponsible worker and poor provider. Louise was his only child, and he was attached to her and concerned with her welfare. As she grew older, this concern focused on her sexual behavior. He set rules and prohibitions about her dating and warned her to come in early and to avoid any indulgence in sexual activity. When she defiantly stayed out late, he would accuse her of promiscuity. Theirs was a relationship of mutual provocation and eroticized argument.

Louise's father died when she was eighteen, and after his death she entered a series of sexual relationships, as though she were acting out her father's fantasies about her promiscuity. Within the year she became pregnant with her first illegitimate child, and two years after that she had a second son out of wedlock.

She met Jack in a bar during her second pregnancy. Jack had been a virtually fatherless boy, and he was very attached to his mother. He bragged to Louise about his sexual exploits, drank heavily, and expressed depreciatory attitudes toward women, but he treated the pregnant Louise with great respect throughout the courtship and made no sexual advances. The child was born and placed out for adoption, and then the Orens had an unusual secret marriage. They went to Nevada for the week end and married under slightly altered names. They returned Sunday night to their respective families because Jack did not want his mother to know about the marriage. They lived apart for almost a year until a second and public wedding ceremony, after which they established a separate household.

Sexual difficulties developed early in the marriage. Mrs. Oren, who had previously enjoyed sex, became frigid and withdrawing; Mr. Oren was demanding and angry. Her sexual disinterest became the focus of persistent concern and argument between them, repeating with some reversals the eroticized quarrels with her father. Eventually the Orens became more distant from one another. Jack worked long hours and when at home would watch television or read the newspaper. Their main contact was in periodic bouts of open recrimination that focused on their dissatisfactions.

Mrs. Oren also had severe conflicts about child-rearing. She had some kind of severe emotional crisis a few months after the birth of her first child and resolved that crisis by going back to work and allowing friends to raise her son. She took him back some time after her marriage but continued to work until her next pregnancy. Several months after the birth of her daughter, Mrs. Oren had another severe emotional crisis. She had become very concerned about her sexual difficulties and was afraid she would get pregnant again; she felt depressed; she worried about going back to the way she had been before marriage. One day she began to cry out that her abdomen was swelling and would burst and she would die. She was hospitalized in a general hospital, treated briefly as an "anxiety state," and released within a week. From this time until the psychotic episode three years later, Mrs. Oren was beset by severe anxieties and various abdominal and gynecological symptoms. She tried to work but was discouraged from so doing by her husband. She became concerned about her relationship to her children as well as by her sexual difficulties with her husband. A real sexual incident in the neighborhood became elaborated into psychotic fantasy, and ideas of reference and feelings of being watched developed. She became concerned about her children's safety and was found giving her daughter mouth-to-mouth artificial respiration. At this point she was hospitalized.

Mrs. Oren was hospitalized for nine weeks and discharged in good remission. She followed up a recommendation for out-patient psychotherapy. Although she frequently missed appointments, she seemed to derive some support from the relationship. Several months after discharge Louise began to feel bored and restless; at first she considered going back to work, but soon her interest focused on having another child. She was pregnant at our last follow-up interview about eighteen months following discharge. In view of her history, it may be that special trouble lies ahead.

ROSE PRICE

At the time of hospitalization Rose Price was thirty-four, and her husband William was about forty-six. They had been married fourteen years and had three sons aged thirteen, eleven, and four. Rose herself was one of a large family which she rarely could describe more fully than as "a big happy bunch." She was the fourth of five children born in her mother's first and father's second marriage; additionally, she had three much older half brothers and sisters. Very little is known of her childhood and early life. Dependency rivalry with the sisters nearest her in age is suggested by memories of having to "work out" and take care of other people while her sisters stayed at home and received care and attention for minor sicknesses. Rose had a few memories of adolescent dating which represent her as graciously stepping aside to yield suitors to less-favored sisters. When she met William, she liked the fact that he was older than the boys she knew and seemed so much more understanding. Initially William viewed her as someone rather helpless and dependent who needed to be rescued from an unhappy family situation.

According to William, Rose was jolly, good-natured, and active during the first part of their marriage. From late in her first pregnancy, however, she began to have crises, characterized as "spells." She would develop multiple and vague physical complaints, would lose interest in housework and later in child care, and would express a need to have someone with her at all times. She usually turned to her mother and older sisters for help. When female relatives were not available, Rose would relentlessly cling to her husband and demand to accompany him to work and elsewhere. After William moved his family to California, Rose went home for maternal care during these intermittent "spells." Later William opposed her frequent trips across country. Gradually he assumed more and more of his wife's household functions, becoming both father and mother to the children as well as caretaker for his wife, and Rose withdrew into further helplessness and inactivity. There was a complicated reciprocity in this arrangement, for William derived distinct gratification from her inadequacy and also from his usurpation of the maternal role. When Rose found part-time work and companionship in a neighbor's home, William induced her to quit. The Prices lived in isolation from neighbors, had no friends, and seldom saw relatives any more. Within the family Mrs. Price became a criticized and depreciated child, actually competing for Mr. Price's maternal affections. In this context a pattern of chronic autism developed and was sustained. Mr. Price increasingly ignored her. In the period before hospitalization Rose became preoccupied with fears that her youngest son would be harmed and clung to the delusion that she was again pregnant.

During her eight-week hospitalization Mr. Price continued to personally assume his wife's domestic and child-care functions, took no initiative to obtain her release, and accepted her eventual return with obvious reluctance. Mrs. Price was rehospitalized three times within thirty-five months of her first release, had spent most of that period in the hospital, and was still in the hospital at our last check. William and his sons had moved away to a farm in a primitive rural area, and the two adolescent boys had quit school to work with their father.

RUTH QUINN

Ruth Quinn was thirty-eight years old, and her husband Tim was thirty-six at the time of her hospitalization. They had been married for over fourteen years and had two children—a boy thirteen and a girl eleven. Ruth herself was the youngest of four daughters. Her father, who died when she was sixteen, was a heavy drinker and a poor provider. Ruth, his favorite daughter, characterized him as emotionally unstable and immature. Her mother is described as harshly critical and interfering, and Ruth claims to have never got along with her. The relationship between the sisters was very close during childhood, and in adult life Ruth depended very much on her sister Ella in particular, turning to her repeatedly for advice and support. Ella was in turn protective, possessive, dominating, and critical toward Ruth.

Ruth entered nurse's training after high school and met Tim while he was a patient. He proposed and she accepted, but several times she thought of backing out during their one-year engagement. Tim was in the service when they finally married, and he did not return home for good until after the birth of their son. Shortly after Tim's return Ruth became pregnant again, and Tim felt trapped and furious toward her. He felt saddled with responsibilities and blocked in his vocational and financial ambitions. She felt guilty, rejected, and very dependent. After the birth of a daughter, Ruth began to drink heavily and compulsively. She gained excessive weight and started to neglect the housework and the children. There were violent quarrels and physical assaults by both partners during this period. Tim also drank heavily. He repeatedly threatened to leave her and actually did so for a few days on several occasions. Ruth made at least three attempts at suicide after violent quarrels with her husband. She saw a physician for help in losing weight, told him some of her feelings and problems, and eventually accepted his suggestion that she join Alcoholics Anonymous. She stopped drinking immediately after joining AA and with few exceptions remained sober over the next four years.

Ruth continued to struggle with her weight. She felt fat and unattractive. Tim was contemptuous of her. She lost a large amount of weight but became increasingly withdrawn, confused, and suspicious. She felt better for a while after her doctor encouraged her and gave her vitamins but soon slumped again. She remained in bed most of the day, and she was convinced that people were talking about her and that strange things were happening. Tim took her to the doctor, ostensibly for a physical ailment, but with the definite intention of having her hospitalized. She was hospitalized and diagnosed as paranoid schizophrenic.

Ruth was hospitalized for five months and received electroshock therapy. She gradually accepted the fact that Tim was going to end the marriage and would not take her back. Her husband made arrangements for the children, and Ruth lived for a time with Ella and then alone in a nearby room. Twenty months after release her situation remained about the same. She was not overtly psychotic, but she lived alone, did not work or have responsibility for her children, and found emotional support and relationship primarily in her dependent, regressive tie to Ella and other female relatives.

ANN RAND

Ann Rand was thirty-six, and her husband Louis was thirty-seven at the time of her hospitalization. This was her second marriage and his first; they had been married for thirteen years. The family had two sons, aged eleven and six, plus Ann's sixteen-year-old son by her first marriage.

Ann was the youngest of eleven children. Her father had had five children by a previous marriage; six more were born in his marriage to Ann's mother. Ann's father had done very well financially earlier in his life, but, by the time Ann was born, he had lost his business and his money and had moved with his family to another state, where he held a number of odd jobs. Her mother had to work from Ann's infancy and was away from home much of the time. The older children fended for themselves and took care of the younger ones. Ann was babied and fussed over by her brothers and sisters, but they also teased her a lot, envied her, and excluded her from many of their activities. Her mother was an eccentric woman, very punitive and rejecting, and she had become a member of a fundamentalist religious sect just before Ann's birth. Ann's mother would not celebrate the pagan rites of Christmas, but Ann's father did make or buy gifts. Her father was particularly fond of Ann, his baby, but the parents could not get along, argued bitterly, and separated when Ann was about six or seven. After that she received gifts from her father and saw him occasionally until he moved far away. He died when Ann was fifteen. Her mother became, if anything, increasingly odd and abusive after her divorce.

Ann married her first husband when she was eighteen, and divorced him three years later after having a son. She said of this marriage only that her husband was very jealous, that he never wanted her to leave the house, and that, when she did so, he would question her in detail. It is not known whether she gave him reason to be jealous. She separated from him several times but did not seek divorce until she had met and planned marriage with Louis Rand. Her first husband wanted custody of the son, and Ann agreed to this.

The Rands married right after her divorce. Louis was a self-contained, even-tempered, conscientious, rather passive man. After the birth of their first son, Ann wanted to regain custody of her other son—then about five—and was able to do so. Another son was born when Ann was thirty, after seven years of marriage. We do not know whether there were any gross personal or marital difficulties during these years, nor do we know why major difficulties became apparent about two years before hospitalization. Ann had been increasingly restive, possibly about her youngest child's leaving babyhood, perhaps in response to an increasing sense of deprivation and isolation in the marriage. In any event, from the time she was about thirty-three, Ann started taking a diffuse series of courses at junior college with some thought about a career out of the home. She began to complain to her physician of gastrointestinal pains, extreme nervousness, and insomnia. As the months passed, she felt herself to be on a merry-go-round; she was too busy but could not stop. She cried a great deal and felt very depressed and guilty. She had sinned, and her past would catch up with her. She had strong fears that she would lose control of herself; she felt unable to respond sexually. These symptoms waxed and waned but generally worsened over a two-year period during which her husband worked overtime, was minimally involved with her and the home, and ignored her difficulties. She was in a panic at the time of hospitalization, very guilt-ridden, and convinced that she would die if she moved her bowels.

Ann reconstituted her defenses quickly at the hospital and was released after only six weeks. She seemed quite brittle, but it was clear that she feared a profound disorganization if she remained away from her family any longer. During hospitalization Louis visited often and expressed genuine concern for Ann's welfare. After hospitalization Louis was more attentive to her, helped out in the home, and expected and demanded less of her. He thus provided somewhat more dependent gratification; she could justify this (to herself) only by her illness and her years of hard work. Ann's posthospital adaptation impressed us as brittle, but quite possibly she had always been so. She was not rehospitalized during a direct follow-up check of more than a year and was apparently free of gross symptoms at that time. A review of records disclosed no rehospitalizations for her in the twenty-eight months following her release.

PEGGY SAND

Peggy Sand was twenty-nine, and her husband Floyd was thirty-six at the time of her hospitalization. This was the only marriage for each of them, and they had been married for twelve years. Their two daughters were eleven and six. Peggy herself was the oldest of eight children. Her family was very poor, moved around a great deal, and sometimes lived in migrant workers' camps. She rarely spoke of her father; the impression is that of a generally quiet, passive, ineffectual man. He died when Peggy was twenty. Her mother was clearly the dominant figure in the family, making the decisions, bossing the children, and complaining of her husband's inability to provide her and the children with the decent things of life. Themes of deprivation were repeatedly expressed by the mother and then by the children in their rivalries.

Peggy was eager to be on her own from her early teens. She was upset by favoritism shown toward her brothers and sisters, and she rebelled against attempts by her mother to control her behavior. She ran around with young people her mother found objectionable, she drank and stayed out to all hours, and she was sexually promiscuous. She was only sixteen when she met Floyd. Floyd had been on his own and learned to take care of himself from early in life; he was a rough, hard-working, hard-driving man with a great deal of suppressed anger. They began to go together, fought a lot, had sexual relations, and married over her mother's objections when Peggy was seventeen. Her mother felt that Peggy was making a big mistake in marrying Floyd, and defiance was undoubtedly a factor in Peggy's motivation to go through with the marriage.

The marriage was sadomasochistic. Peggy repeatedly provoked her husband into a fury by stubborn defiance, by secretly spending for herself money given to her to pay bills, and by arousing his jealousy. They would have bitter fights, and he would beat her; their sexual relations were also characterized by resistance and attack. He sometimes came home drunk and created a scene. Very often Peggy left him after quarrels. In the first years of the marriage, she repeatedly went home to her mother; later she went to a sister's or a friend's home. One separation several months after the birth of their first child lasted nearly a year, during which time Peggy stayed with her mother and dying father. But most of the separations were brief and seemed a part of the sadomasochistic interaction. In contrast to superficially similar processes in some separation crisis cases, in which we believe the wife turned to her mother out of guilt and out of feelings of intense emptiness and panic when unsupported by the husband, Peggy turned from her husband during quarrels primarily to demonstrate mistreatment at his hands and to punish him. Peggy also threatened divorce on a number of occasions and actually began proceedings once, charging her husband with extreme cruelty. The judge urged reconciliation and recommended they seek psychiatric help. Mrs. Sand visited a psychiatrist a few times, but she did not consider it helpful and stopped.

Peggy was not a zealous mother, and Floyd complained about having to help out with child care. He thought that she did not keep close enough track of the children. It is not clear to what extent Peggy herself experienced any distress about being a mother early in the marriage, but for unknown reasons she did make some kind of suicidal gesture shortly after her first child was born, and her one long marital separation also occurred at about this time. She later complained that the children were too much for her and threatened to turn herself over to a mental hospital because they upset her so. The thought of going to a mental hospital to get away or to get help began to occur to her a couple of years before her hospitalization, but it is unclear how distressed she felt. She often felt upset, cried, had trouble sleeping, was depressed, and began to feel helpless and alone. There is no evidence that she experienced at this time (or any later time) the degree of immobilization or agitation found in the other women we studied or that she ever had any psychotic ideation. Her husband ignored and ridiculed her various complaints and shortly before her hospitalization switched to a job which took him out of the home most of the time except for sleeping. The impression is that patterns of mutual withdrawal had begun to replace chronic battling. The immediate precipitation of hospitalization, however, was a furious argument between the Sands. Mrs. Sand felt insulted and violently angry. Perhaps she also felt afraid. In any event, she got into the family car, drove herself to the state mental hospital without informing her husband or anyone else of her plans, and asked for voluntary admission, stating that she felt very upset and feared she might harm someone.

The hospitalization was stormy. Mr. Sand was convinced his wife had gone to the hospital simply to spite him, and he threatened to retaliate by committing her or never coming to visit her or keeping the children from her. Peggy meanwhile began a courtship with a male patient she met at a recreational activity, smuggled letters back and forth to him, and eventually managed a week-end rendezvous in a nearby town under circumstances guaranteed to come to the attention of her husband. He was furious, decided she must be insane to do such a thing, and sought her commitment. Meanwhile, the hospital staff had been drawn into various crosscurrents by Peggy and Floyd, and there was considerable staff confusion and conflict over how Peggy should be diagnosed and whether she should be committed. In brief, she was diagnosed as schizophrenic, undifferentiated, and was committed. The length of hospitalization was about nineteen weeks. Sixteen months later, at the time of our last direct follow-up check, Mrs. Sand was still married and living at home. She had no conspicuous symptoms and had not been rehospitalized, but so far as we could determine neither she nor the marriage had changed from the pathological prehospital patterns.

CORA THORNE

Cora and Peter Thorne had been married for nine years at the time of her hospitalization. Mrs. Thorne was just thirty-one, and her husband Peter was a few months older. The Thornes had three children—a seven-year-old daughter and a five-year-old and an eleven-month-old son.

Cora was the third of four children. Her father was a passive, ineffectual, and remote man toward whom she did not develop a close relationship. In discussing her childhood, she rarely mentioned him spontaneously. Cora's mother was overprotective and obsessed with the idea that something dangerous might happen to her children. Cora's older brother became very disturbed and aggressive in adolescence and was hospitalized as psychotic.

Cora was an anxious, compliant, rather dependent girl who saw herself as uninteresting and unattractive. She did not have many boy friends and was very flattered when Peter began to take an interest in her. Apparently the first months of their marriage were relatively happy and trouble free for Cora, but, from the time of the first pregnancy, she became anxious, withdrew from sexual relations, was reluctant to go out with her husband, could not tolerate being alone, and turned repeatedly to her mother. Mr. Thorne was at first disturbed by these changes, but later he accepted them and finally encouraged her regressive dependence upon mother. The Thornes lived in increasingly separate worlds. Peter found occasion to go to work six or seven days a week, and he sought companionship and recreation with work colleagues. Cora became preoccupied with the children in a worried, overprotective, and irritable way, and she spoke lengthily with her mother each day. On one occasion Cora phoned her mother in the morning and arranged to speak with her again that afternoon. Her mother was out when she called back. Cora became quite upset and could hardly restrain herself from checking hospitals or calling the police to find out about her mother.

Cora's unexpected third pregnancy made Peter feel trapped, and he began to go out with another woman. A few months before hospitalization Peter told Cora of this affair and of his intention of divorcing her. Cora was frightened and desperate, fantasied that it was all a test and that her husband really loved her, developed the conviction that she was again pregnant, and, as time went on, became fearful of plots by her husband and others to kill her or the children. She tried to take her own life, but she was not hospitalized until she attacked one of her children.

During the hospital period Peter was initially uncertain of his plans, but he finally decided to proceed with a separation and eventual divorce. Cora gradually came to accept the inevitable. She received electroshock therapy and was released in fairly good remission after twenty-nine weeks. At first she lived alone near her mother, and Peter kept the children. Cora began to work and found this satisfying. Peter took her out on "dates." A short time later they were reconciled. Cora continued to work and allowed a housekeeper to care for the children. She seemed much happier, less anxious, and less withdrawn than she had been for many years. The last follow-up information is from about sixteen months after release, and there had been no rehospitalization or further changes in Cora's life.

DONNA UREY

At the time of her hospitalization, Donna Urey was twenty-six, and her husband Albert was twenty-seven. They had been married eight years and had five children. Donna's own childhood was characterized by extreme neglect, abuse, and chaos. She related very little of it to us, emphasizing that what is past is past and should be forgotten; however, much of her early life became accessible through records of the social agencies who dealt with Donna and her parents over the years. Donna was the first of five children born to parents who did not marry until several years after her birth. Two other children were also born out of wedlock. Donna's father was an erratic and irresponsible man, often in trouble with the law. Her mother did not keep house or watch the children very much or very well. The children lived in filth and squalor and were frequently whipped. The police found them begging in stores or wandering about the business area of town and brought them home. Donna came to school dirty and hungry and behaved there poorly and untruthfully. The father abandoned the family for good when Donna was six. The mother abandoned the children by asking a social agency to take over because she could not take care of them when she (the mother) was twenty-six and Donna was eight.

In the following years Donna lived in a Catholic orphanage and then with a series of foster mothers. In each setting Donna initially behaved in a helpful and appealing way, was well liked, experienced the foster mother as nurturant, and felt that she had found a woman who treated her as a mother should. During such periods Donna seemed transformed. For example, in contrast to early descriptions of her schooling, one high school report card showed an A in citizenship and in several academic courses, with an over-all B average. But after a time in each foster home, Donna would experience the new mother as depriving, would become disobedient, and would run away. In each instance she ran toward a new home where she had already begun to form a new maternal attachment and where she believed she would find a good mother.

Donna met Albert in high school, formed a close and warm relationship with his mother, and was taken into their home. She later eloped with Albert against his mother's wishes. A reconciliation with her mother-in-law was eventually achieved. Like so many of the foster home placements, the marriage was initially very successful, and Donna blossomed. But after she began to have children, she started to feel lonely and neglected, her formerly excellent housekeeping deteriorated, she occasionally wandered away from home, and she may have had some sexual escapades. After a time she began to hear voices accusing her of not properly caring for her children. Her experience of neglect and deprivation and the projected reproaches about her own mothering seem to replicate the anger she felt toward her own neglectful mother and her own sense of deprivation as a child. Mrs. Urey was overtly psychotic for several years before hospitalization. She told her husband she needed to leave, could not manage things, and belonged in a hospital, but he told her she was not "that bad off." Donna was hospitalized at age twenty-six, when she set fire to her home and said that she could no longer manage the care of her children. This was her mother's age at the time Donna was abandoned. At the time of hospitalization Mrs. Urey had five children; her oldest, a daughter, was eight. At the time of Donna's earlier abandonment, she was eight and the oldest of five children.

Donna's hospital stay was longer than any other first hospitalization in the study group. She was given electroshock therapy and finally placed on indefinite leave sixty-four weeks after admission. She was rehospitalized about a year and a half after release in about the same condition as before and was still in the hospital at our final contact two months later.

RITA VICK

At the time of hospitalization Rita Vick was twenty-nine, and her husband Leo was thirty-six. They had been living together for almost four years and had been legally married for about three years. They had two sons, aged two and one. Rita had been married three times previously, including one common-law marriage. She had had six children by four men prior to this marriage. Leo had been married once before.

Rita was born out of wedlock when her mother was sixteen, and she lived with her grandparents until she was three, when her mother married. The mother's marriage remained intact, and Rita had two stepbrothers and one stepsister. From the age of five, when the first stepbrother was born, Rita's behavior became very difficult. She constantly told lies "in order to get attention." She would steal things, sometimes turning them over to her mother as gifts. At times she would "run away to Granny" when there was trouble. Later she stayed out of school often and lied about it to her parents. She was often in trouble for her behavior and her lying, and Rita reports that she was frequently beaten by both her mother and her stepfather. (It should be mentioned that at various times Rita gave us contradictory accounts of her life; as it happens, many events in her disturbed adult life became the concern of social agencies, probation departments, the police, and the courts, and were recorded independently by other observers at the time.)

Rita quit school in the seventh grade. It is unclear what she did between then and age nineteen, when she ran off and married a sailor, returning home pregnant while her husband went to sea. Her husband returned shortly before the birth of their son, Tony, and the family moved to another state. Rita's husband then re-enlisted and shipped out to sea again. Rita began running around with other men, leaving her infant son without care. She was arrested and convicted of child neglect, and Tony was placed in temporary custody of Rita's mother. Later Rita's husband returned, and they established a home, taking Tony with them. Marital troubles developed, however. Rita and Tony went to live with her mother for a whole, and then Rita obtained a divorce.

Rita remarried within a year, giving birth to a son a few months afterward. Over the next three years she gave birth to twin sons and apparently also a daughter by another man. Her husband was away for long periods of time (he also was a seaman), and in his absence she was promiscuous. He divorced her and obtained legal custody of his three children. We are unable to determine the disposition of the illegitimate daughter.

Rita took up residence with another man and became pregnant again. The man left her long before the child was born, but he acknowledged paternity and paid her a monthly sum for child support. During this pregnancy Rita frequently left Tony alone. One night the five-year-old boy was turned over to a policeman by a janitor who had discovered him alone in a theater at 1:00 in the morning. After an investigation which revealed several earlier instances of similar neglect, the child was placed in a foster home. A month later Rita gave birth to Ronald and immediately had him placed in a foster home.

Rita was twenty-five when she met Leo Vick. They met in a bar and began to live together within a week. Leo had been married to a woman who had been previously married more than once and who was frequently unfaithful to him. He recalled how nervous and unhappy Rita seemed when he met her and how terrible she felt about the loss of Tony. He knew that many people considered Rita a bad girl, but he did not. "The way I saw it, she just put faith in the wrong kind of men." Mr. Vick was steadily employed, and the couple soon moved into a home of their own. Rita frequently visited Tony in his foster home, and with her husband's support she took formal steps to regain custody of the child. A psychologist who examined Rita on behalf of the court characterized her as extremely unstable, as someone who could approach psychosis when her plans went awry. The psychologist said that she was making sincere but superficial efforts to control her behavior in order to get Tony back. Her first husband (Tony's father) had since remarried, was actively opposed to Rita's obtaining control of the child, and sought custody himself. The court gave the father temporary custody, and he took the boy to his home in a distant state. Rita was violently upset in court and afterward. She would not eat, she cried, she carried kitchen knives around and hinted that she would kill herself, and she threatened to run away from home. Leo called the police, and Rita was hospitalized in the psychiatric ward of the county hospital in what appeared to be a state of agitated depression. Although initially violent on the ward, she calmed down in a few days and was released in less than a week.

This episode occurred almost three years prior to her admission to the state hospital. During the three years Rita gave continuing evidence of distress at the loss of Tony and made further efforts to obtain custody. She believed that her early placement of Ronald had influenced the adverse decision about Tony, and, although she had shown no previous interest in Ronald, she began to consider requesting that he be returned to her. Meanwhile she had given birth to her first son in her present marriage. Immediately following a Probation Department recommendation that Tony's return to Mrs. Vick be deferred until further investigation of her plans for her other children, especially Ronald, Mrs. Vick requested that Ronald be returned to her care. A month after Ronald returned, he had to be hospitalized in a very battered and bruised condition after an "accident" which roused suspicions that he had been beaten. Mrs. Vick's account of the accident frequently changed. The child proved to be severely brain-damaged. It was at about this time that Mrs. Vick gave birth to another son. A few months later a court hearing gave custody of Ronald, who had been hospitalized, to his former foster parents and concluded that the investigation of the injury had begun too late to determine its actual cause. Mrs. Vick protested furiously that it was all the fault of the former foster parents and that the child really had been unwell when returned to her.

It will come as no surprise that the marital relationship between the Vicks had become troubled. Mr. Vick sought help for himself at a family service agency. When a final court hearing gave Tony's custody to the father, Rita reacted to this decision with fury, had violent rages and tantrums, and threatened to kill all of the people in the various agencies. One night she called the police and asked an officer to take her to the hospital because she was crazy and had to get out of the house. The officer said he could not take her, but about two weeks later she went with Leo to a mental hygiene clinic and made arrangements for voluntary admission to the state hospital. She was diagnosed as schizophrenic reaction.

At first Mrs. Vick was very agitated in the hospital and was sent to the locked ward. She received drug therapy and electro-shock therapy, improved, went home on several visits, and failed to return from a visit about thirteen weeks after admission. Difficulties continued at home, however, and she voluntarily returned to the hospital. She received some group and individual therapy, was reported to be doing well, failed to return from another visit, and was formally discharged as improved.

The Vicks moved several times in the ensuing months. Once, during a fight between Rita and Leo, he called the police and had her taken to county hospital where she remained for only two days. About a year later she gave birth to a girl, her third child in this marriage. Six weeks later Leo left her, taking the children with him, and filed divorce papers which alleged that Rita beat their one-month-old baby on the body and face and threw her against the wall. He sought custody of the children. Our last follow-up information was about two years after Rita's first release. She was not in the hospital. She was living alone but was involved in an obscure relationship with a policewoman friend and an untrained "psychologist" who were helping her with her problems by hypnotism.

KATE WHITE

At the time of her hospitalization, Kate White was thirty-six, and her husband Nelson was thirty-eight. They had been married for twelve years and had two daughters aged five and two. Kate herself was the second of two daughters. Her older sister was a docile and obedient girl who was quite clearly her mother's favorite. Kate was her father's favorite, and she identified with him in many ways. She became a tomboy, active, outspoken, and rebellious. She later pursued career interests similar to his.

Kate's father carried on a long-standing affair with his secretary, but the parents had decided to remain together, ostensibly for the sake of the children. The affair was initially kept from the children, although they had reason to suspect it. When Kate was eight or nine, her mother openly confronted the daughters with their father's infidelity and made a direct bid for their sympathy and allegiance against father. Kate vowed to herself not to become a suffering martyr like her mother. Her father's affair also intensified the erotic implications of Kate's attachment to him. In Kate's adolescence and even in her young adulthood, her father was jealous and possessive and actively intervened to block her relations with men.

After college and a brief period of employment, Kate hesitantly accepted the proposal of a young man who had the same career interests that she and her father shared. Their life was rootless for some time as Nelson tried to find himself, and Kate's role was initially that of a competent career woman. Feminine domestic activities did not come easily and provided her with little sense of satisfaction and pride. Later, when she had children, she felt hopelessly tied down and frustrated in her career aspirations and guilty about these feelings. She began to have a recurrent idea that her husband was homosexual. Sometimes she also suspected him of infidelity, and she often felt intensely tempted to have affairs. Her one actual affair was deeply disturbing to her.

Kate's severe personality disorganization began shortly after the Whites bought their first home and experienced a sense that, after more than a decade of marriage, they were really settling down. At the time of the episode itself, Kate's marital family repeated many significant features of her parental family. The marital family consisted of two daughters, a father whose work kept him away from home much of the time, and a mother who felt martyred in her role. Some of Kate's symptoms reflected a reliving of some distressing aspects of her own childhood through identification with her children: she felt her daughters had come into possession of some terrible information which they had not been meant to know and that this knowledge would cause them harm; they seemed to be giving her "signs" that indicated that she should leave her husband. Kate resolved that she must not burden the children with her troubles as she herself had been burdened by her mother, but she was preoccupied with how the precarious condition of her marriage would affect them. Other symptoms mirrored her own erotic attachment to and identification with her father. She was preoccupied with guilt about her actual extramarital affair as well as about fantasies of having affairs and with suspicions that her husband was unfaithful. When the psychiatrist she saw briefly before hospitalization replaced his secretary, Kate believed that he did this in order to have an affair with her. Religious ideation and protestations about the "sanctity of marriage" expressed a guilt-dominated identification with her mother. Thoughts about her husband's hypothetical homosexuality expressed her own confused sexual identity.

Mrs. White was hospitalized for about twenty-nine weeks. She wore hospital clothing, which was not required; resisted visits home; and expressed reluctance to see her children. Very gradually her symptoms abated, and she returned to her husband and children. The Whites vowed to try to settle down and "really live like a married couple for the first time." Earlier discords reappeared, however, and each partner withdrew into his own concerns. Mrs. White became promiscuous for a time. She was rehospitalized briefly fifteen months after release and for a period of several months beginning eighteen months after release. At the last follow-up interview, two years after the first release, Mrs. White was on leave from the state hospital, her husband was having an extramarital affair with his secretary (thus replicating the childhood drama), and the couple agreed on virtually nothing other than that their marriage had disintegrated and was maintained only for the sake of appearances. Mrs. White was in a partial remission which seemed quite brittle.

MARY YALE

At the time of her hospitalization, Mary Yale was twenty-nine, and her husband George was thirty-four. They had been married for over five years and had a daughter almost four. Mary was herself the younger of two children. Her older brother had been her father's pride, had been pushed a great deal, and had always seemed able and successful. Throughout childhood Mary was openly but impotently rivalrous toward him. Her father's family role, apart from his interest in his son, did not emerge clearly; occupationally he was always dissatisfied, falling short of his aspirations and feeling he was somehow in the wrong line of work. Mary was very close to her mother, and, after her father's death during her teens, the two women became more dependent on each other. While her brother was away at school, Mary and her mother lived together in an apartment. Mary's mother did all the housework and cooking, even washing her daughter's clothes and hair. The mother enjoyed and counted on being helpful to her daughter, but Mary felt caught in and stifled by this relationship, unable to assume much responsibility, to do much for herself, or to form attachments which would threaten the maternal tie.

Mary fled home at twenty-four—"I had to get away from there." She felt scared and empty on her own, met George Yale, and rushed into marriage. George was a lonely, drifting bachelor who had moved from job to job and from transient involvement to transient involvement. He did not like to feel tied down. He had never expected to marry but somehow did so at this time. Within two weeks of marriage George lost his job and moved cross country with his bride to live with her mother. Later they moved to a separate apartment nearby, but Mary continued to see her mother almost daily. Throughout the marriage Mary moved back and forth, in both physical and emotional space, between mother and husband. Later, faced on the one hand with a deterioration and the threatened loss of her husband and with increasing claims by her mother on the other hand, Mrs. Yale felt she could not go on. The episode began by Mary's crying quietly for hours. She would angrily reject her mother and then cling to her; she would desperately cling to her husband but reject intimacy with him; she became exaggeratedly protective toward her child and feared that harm would befall the little girl. She began to develop homosexual preoccupations and delusions. An attempt at psychotherapy foundered on her own guilt, her mother's resentment of a competing relationship, and her husband's passive resistance to the treatment.

Mary Yale was hospitalized for eighteen weeks and received electroshock therapy. During the hospitalization the Yales agreed to try to make their marriage work and to seek more independence from her mother. But within a week of Mary's release, *Mr.* Yale was anxious and irritable, felt that his wife was too dependent on him, and began to withdraw. The Yales separated a few months later, and Mary and her child moved in with her mother. Later the marital partners were again reconciled. Two years after release Mrs. Yale was working and contributing significantly to the support of the family; she was also finding much emotional gratification in her job. She was living with her husband and retained some emotional distance from her mother, who lived nearby. She had not been rehospitalized and was free of obvious psychiatric symptoms.

Index

C

childhood roles, 21, 31, 64–66, 119
CONOVER, GLENN C., 73, 73n.,
    121n.
CORNELISON, ALICE, 119n.
crises, adolescent; *see* schizophre-
    nia, and adolescence
crises, identification; *see* identifi-
    cation crises
crises, schizophrenic; *see* schizo-
    phrenia
crises, separation; *see* separation
    crises
crises, transition; *see* identification
    crises; separation crises
crisis resolutions, 95–116; *see also*
    deviance, accommodation to
CUMMING, ELAINE, 128, 128n.
CUMMING, JOHN, 128, 128n.

D

data-collection, 15–19, 117–118
    interviewers' responsibilities, 15
    interviews
        frequency, 16–18
        nature, 15–16
        observations, 15–16
        records, types used, 15
    results
        analysis of, 18–19, 117–118
        disguise of cases, 18
        raw materials, 18
DAVIS, JAMES A., 73n.
DAY, JULIANA, 119n.
DEASY, LEILA CALHOUN, 7n., 73n.,
    121n.
deviance
    accommodation to, 73–89, 121–
        125; *see also* individual
        cases
    mutual withdrawal, 63, 75–83,
        96, 107–114

disruption of, 83, 88, 107–
    108
and family's posthospital re-
    organization, 108–114
husband's role, 78–82
and identification cases, 115
and professional care, 78, 88,
    122–123
tolerance of, 73, 79, 88–89
triadic overinvolvement, 83–87,
    96, 98–107
disruption of, 84, 86–87, 89
and family's posthospital re-
    organization, 99–107
and professional care, 85–89,
    123
and separation cases, 116
documentation, method of, 19

E

ENGLE, BERNICE, 4n., 124n.

F

family, contemporary; *see also*
    marital family; parental
    family
and identification crises; *see*
    identification crises
and personal stability; *see*
    marital family
and professional care, 6–7
and separation crises; *see* sepa-
    ration crises
as social-control device, 73–74,
    87–89, 122–125
family's posthospital reorganiza-
    tion; *see also* individual
    cases
in identification cases, 115
in mutual withdrawal cases,
    108–114
in separation cases, 115–116

in triadic overinvolvement cases, 99–07
father, role of
in separation cases, 34, 49
feminine identity; *see* schizophrenia
FISK, FERN, 51*n.*
FLECK, STEPHEN, 20, 20*n.*, 32*n.*, 119*n.*
FREEMAN, EDITH H., 123*n.*
FREEMAN, HOWARD E., 7*n.*, 73*n.*
FREUD, SIGMUND, 22, 22*n.*

G

GOFFMAN, ERVING, 72*n.*
GREENSON, RALPH R., 51, 51*n.*

H

HALEY, JAY, 119*n.*
HARRIS, ROBERT, 123*n.*
HILGARD, JOSEPHINE R., 51, 51*n.*, 59
HILL, LEWIS B., 32, 32*n.*
HIRSCH, STANLEY, 119*n.*
hospitalization
as social process, 72–74, 97, 105–107
husband; *see also* individual cases
in identification cases, 66
in mutual withdrawal, 75–83, 109–112
in separation cases, 34
and symbiosis, 34
and triadic overinvolvement, 83–87, 102, 104–105

I

identification crises, 50–66, 96, 119
and anniversary reactions, 51, 59, 61, 63

and contemporary family processes, 50, 59, 63
and personal stability, 63
content of identifications, 59, 65–66
and mother-child relationship, 50, 59
interviews; *see* data-collection

J

JACKSON, DON D., 6*n.*, 20*n.*, 32*n.*, 119*n.*
James case, 59–61, 75, 93–94, 135–137
accommodation to deviance, 75
adaptation to marital tasks, 59–61
children's role, 60
family's posthospital reorganization, 94
husband's role, 60
marital family, structure of, 60–61
mother's role, 60–61
parental family, structure of, 60
personal posthospital adjustment, wife's, 93–94

K

KALIS, BETTY, 123, 123*n.*
Karr case, 31, 39–42, 83, 85, 87, 95, 101, 103–104, 119–120, 137–139
accommodation to deviance, 83, 85
accommodation to marital tasks,
functions of, 41–42
merger with parental family, 39
adaptation to marital tasks, 31, 39–42

For Product Safety Concerns and Information please contact our EU
representative GPSR@taylorandfrancis.com
Taylor & Francis Verlag GmbH, Kaufingerstraße 24, 80331 München, Germany

* 9 7 8 0 2 0 2 3 0 8 1 6 6 *